At The Edge

A Jewish Outsider Finds Her Way

Personal Essays by

Judith A. Goren

ISBN-10: 1461034612
EAN-13: 9781461034612

Published by Sunrise Press
Printed by Createspace

Cover photo: *The author with her family. Left to right: Herman Wise, Judy (10),
Evelyn and Richard (6). Detroit: Palmer Park, 1943.*

Acknowledgements

I want to give special thanks to friends and family who read some or all of this work in earlier stages and provided me with helpful feedback:

My husband, **Bob**, who eagerly read every chapter as it rolled out of the printer, as well as later versions. Because he had lived though most of the events with me, from college years on, his memories as an eye witness were unique, as well as his years of experience as a writer, editor and journalist and his steady support and encouragement as I worked on the manuscript.

My editor, **Gail Waldstein, MD**: doctor, poet, essayist, editor; also author of a book-length memoir, *To Quit this Calling*. We found each other through a mutual friend, and although we live in different cities and have never met in person, we developed a warm and caring relationship via e-mail and phone conversations. Her eye and ear for structure, organization, consistency, rhythm and clarity, as well as avoiding clichéd language, repetition of subject matter and a few dozen other issues that improve writing, added greatly to this manuscript. She not only pointed out what was amiss but also what was done well and what really moved her.

My grandson, **Rob Goren**, for interior and cover design and technical assistance. His creativity and help were invaluable.

My son, **Steven Goren**, for sharing his family archive of photos and for his availability to answer technical questions at the most inconvenient times; my friend, **Ruth Ann Prag Carter**, for her time, energy, astute proofreading and loyal friendship; my team at CreateSpace, and the writer-friends and family members who read and critiqued early versions of individual chapters.

ALSO BY JUDITH A. GOREN

Sharing the Journey: A Psychotherapist Reflects on her Work
(Personal essays) 2004

The Tao of Awakening (poetry chapbook) 1998

Traveling toward the Heart (poems) 1994

Coming Alive (poems) 1975

Inclusions in anthologies:

A Life of Courage: Sherwin Wine and Humanistic Judaism
"The Birthing of Humanistic Judaism: an Eyewitness Account" (2003)
Passages North Anthology: Poems (1990)
Contemporary Michigan Poetry: Poetry from the Third Coast (1988)

Inclusions in literary journals and reviews:

Green River Review, Beloit Poetry Journal, Centennial Review, Echoes from the Moon, Moving Out, Reflections from the Edge, The Bridge, The Maguffin, Humanistic Judaism, Wayne Review, The University of Windsor Review, A Change in Weather, Anthology of Women Poets, Poet: an International Monthly, The Driftwood Review, Ambassador Poetry Project, Redbook, Jewish Currents, The Michigan Poet

Awards:

Detroit Working Writers 110th Anniversary and Spring Readings Awards (2010): Poetry, first and second place awards; Creative non-fiction, first place for "Sunlight and Gifts," the final chapter in *At the Edge.*

At The Edge is dedicated to two outstanding mentors and guides:

Julia Press, *a woman of vastly expanded consciousness, loving- kindness and wisdom, as well as my beloved personal friend, and*

Rabbi Sherwin T. Wine*, of recent memory: teacher, visionary and founder of Secular Humanistic Judaism, now an accepted alternative movement in dozens of countries.*

Each of them continues to have a profound impact on my life, as well as the lives of hundreds of others around the globe.

Contents

At The Edge

A Jewish Outsider Finds Her Way

Preface

❧

By the time I thought of the questions I wish I had asked my grandparents about their lives, they were long gone; so were my parents, aunts and uncles. I noticed, at about the same time, that my grandchildren had never asked me any questions. That led me to thoughts about how different my childhood was from theirs and I decided to write some personal essays for them about my early years. As writing has a way of doing, the story evolved beyond my original intention; the number of things I wanted to write about grew and grew and marched into my adolescence and adulthood.

While my story is not specifically about Detroit, the city is a backdrop, a silent character, in most of these chapters. Detroit may have a bad reputation today (when my husband and I travel the world and folks ask where we're from, we often say vaguely, "southeast Michigan," to avoid raised eyebrows) but that was not true during the years I was growing up.

The Detroit where I lived from my birth in 1933, until my husband was drafted in 1956 and we were transported to France, was a city to live in with pride. Majestic elm trees formed archways across residential streets. Lawns were green and well-kept. City parks were safe, accessible and well cared for: family picnics at Palmer Park, the city swimming pool at Rouge Park and Sunday outings to Belle Isle, on the Detroit River, were all part of my childhood landscape.

The architecture of downtown skyscrapers, built in the 1920's when profits from the automobile industry were booming, was famous around the country. The layout of downtown streets, built around a central point and fanning out like spokes of a wheel, earned Detroit the label "Paris of the West." The Washington Boulevard Historic District was lined with elegant shops. Going downtown to shop at the J.L. Hudson Company Department Store was an exciting excursion into a world that seemed to hold everything. Hudson's occupied a square block with its main entrance on Woodward Avenue. It was 14 stories high; the toy department alone occupied the entire 12th floor. Elevators were operated by white-gloved, uniformed women who sat on folding seats as they rode up and down all day long. Shopping there with my mother was a special occasion for which we dressed up.

Downtown movie theaters, the Fox and the Palm State, were unbelievably lavish in their interior architecture, as was the Fisher Building, a tall, beautifully designed office structure on West Grand Boulevard, just north of the downtown area. Located midway between downtown and the Fisher Building, the Detroit Institute of Arts boasted a mural by the Mexican artist Diego Rivera; my father, then art and music critic for the Detroit Free Press, interviewed him while the work was in progress, shortly before I was born.

Detroit was a city of large brick homes. While there were some apartment buildings, they were not the chief residences for most of the population. The homes ranged from single (for one family) to two-family and four-family flats. The flats were solid, two story buildings with porches both upstairs and downstairs, where people sat on warm summer evenings to enjoy the air and watch neighbors stroll by.

It was also a city of ethnic and class neighborhoods, connected by a network of streetcars (electric trolleys that had wires above and tracks below) and a moderately efficient public bus system. Woodward Avenue divided the city into east and west. The wealthy lived in single homes in Palmer Woods, or on Chicago and Boston Boulevards, or in Grosse Pointe, far away from us on the east side of Detroit. There were several large Polish neighborhoods where many auto workers settled. African-Americans (called, in those days, Negroes) lived in smaller dwellings along Hastings and Brush streets, just east of Woodward Avenue and close to downtown. That neighborhood had once been Jewish and was where my mother grew up. In fact, most Jewish neighborhoods throughout Detroit became black neighborhoods as the Jews moved further northwest in the city. A large kosher market called Dexter-Davison Meats kept those street names over decades as it relocated twice, the last move into a Jewish suburb northwest of Detroit.

When I was growing up, most Jews lived in flats on the west side between Twelfth Street and Dexter, in an area that ran from south of Clairmount to Davison. My parents rented a flat that was at the edge of this neighborhood, a block to the east of Twelfth Street and south of Clairmount, where the homes were a little larger and the neighborhood a mixture of Jew and Gentile. Feeling I was an outsider at the edge of the "real" Jewish community became a theme in my life for many decades.

At the time I was born, the population of Detroit was over a million and a half people, making it the 4th largest city in the United States. The rise of the automobile industry and the availability of jobs in auto factories brought in a huge influx of workers from other states, especially from the south. During World War II, the factories stopped making cars, instead turning out tanks, jeeps and bombers. Detroit became known as the Arsenal of Democracy. After the war, businesses flourished and new neighborhoods grew up as the city expanded.

There were troubles brewing that led to the demise of Detroit but they are not in the scope of this story. As a child I was unaware of the racial and ethnic tensions that would later erupt into riots between black and white. Until high school, when it hit our assimilated family, I was also unaware of the public anti-Semitism fueled by community leaders such as Henry Ford and Father Coughlin, a local priest with a radio program as his forum. I lived comfortably and naively in our upstairs flat, played outdoors with other children on the block, walked safely to school and enjoyed family outings in the city. The Detroit I knew was a pleasant place in which to come of age.

The stories I have chosen to write are those that grabbed me by the shoulders as I looked backward in time. This book falls somewhere between a memoir and a loosely connected series of personal essays. (My concept of "book" is traditional: a three dimensional object that can be held, with pages to be turned by hand. By the time my great-grandchildren arrive, that non-electronic paper artifact may be of more historical interest to them than its contents.) Along the way, the focus of my essays shifted from childhood stories for my grandchildren to the "Jewish outsider" theme of the sub-title. The text marched across the city further than I had planned, and I let it lead me where it needed to go. Along the way I gained new insights into my early years with my parents, my complex relationship with each of them and with my Jewish heritage.

I headed into the unknown. For me, that is the true excitement of writing.

Childhood

∾

Judy (age 3)

The Upstairs Flat

∾

The April I turned four, a few weeks before my brother was born, I held my mother's hand as we walked to visit our new house. My head came just to her tummy, which was big and round. I wore my new saddle shoes and light blue spring coat. The snow had melted and the weather was warmer. There was a fresh smell in the air; Mother noticed it and said that it was the smell of spring.

My parents were moving from our small rented flat to a larger one, two blocks west, on Virginia Park between Woodrow Wilson and Twelfth Street. The new building housed two families, with a full living space on each floor. From the front porch, the outer door opened into a large hallway. To the left was a door leading into the downstairs flat. Straight ahead was a staircase, leading up to our new home. On our walk, mother carried a tape measure, to check the sizes of the rooms for rugs and the windows for curtains. She sang as she measured, while I played games with the sun and shadows on the bare wood floors.

After she was done measuring, mother showed me all the bedrooms. She was especially excited about a room in the very back of the house, which she called the sunroom. There were three large windows on each of the outer walls, facing out over the backyard. "I think Daddy and I will sleep here," she said, "and we'll put the new baby in the room next to this one."

We walked toward the front of the house, down what seemed like a very long hallway. There was a bathroom and two more bedrooms. "You can sleep in either one of these rooms," Mother said. "How about the big one, right here?" I was happy.

That was my room, for a long time. It held my bed, a dresser, shelves with my books and toys and, later, games and my own radio. It was the room that harbored me when I was home from school with a fever; the room where I played jacks on the floor while listening to "Jack Armstrong" and "A Date with Judy" on the radio. It was the room where I could shut the door and tell secrets with my girlfriends, where I sat at my desk to write in my diary and which I used as my refuge when I was unhappy.

In our large dining room, we gathered around the big oak table every night for dinner and every Sunday morning for breakfast with Grandpa Apple, my mother's father. The white stucco ceiling of the dining room had, at its edges, a frieze of plaster fruit, which I studied endlessly. There was a long buffet against one wall. In it was a drawer where my father kept candy. Like all his drawers, everything inside was lined up precisely. There was usually a box of Sander's chocolates, as well as some wrapped hard candies and sometimes a Hershey bar. Although I was allowed to open the drawer and look, I had to ask permission before taking any. When my brother was still a baby, his playpen was also kept in the dining room, so that mother could keep an eye on him from the kitchen.

The breakfast nook, a compact area between dining room and kitchen, was a cozy place to eat breakfast and lunch, as well as bedtime snacks. It housed a table with built-in benches on either side. The table was covered with oilcloth, less formal and easier to clean than the white linen tablecloths Mother used in the dining room.

The kitchen itself was a large rectangular room where Mother spent many hours cooking and washing dishes. A gas stove with an upper oven, a small refrigerator and a toaster were our only appliances. Every Friday, Mother scrubbed the large gray linoleum floor, kneeling on a rubber pad with a bucket of soapy water beside her. After the scrubbing, she rinsed the floor with clear water and a rag, and then wiped up the moisture with another rag. When the floor was done, she spread out newspapers across the length of the room to be walked on until it had thoroughly dried. Washing the floor was a job she hated, and everyone was careful not to bring in dirt or grass on their shoes that day.

A back stairway off the kitchen led down two flights to the basement, where the hot water heater was located. In order to have hot water upstairs, the heater had to be turned on. It was too expensive to keep it on full time, so one parent would have to run down so we could wash dishes and take baths, and then remember to go back to turn it off later. The basement also had a wringer washer and two long rows of clothesline. Each item of clothing had to be hand-turned through the wringer, shaken out and hung up with clothespins on the line to dry. My father hung a swing there so that I could play while my mother did laundry. Even so, I did not like the dark basement with its musty smell of damp cotton. It had a cold cement floor and too many spooky corners. I was happy when we reemerged into daylight.

Every room in the house had a radiator: a large, dark gray metal object that gave off heat in cold weather. It was necessary to be cautious around this monster, as getting close enough to touch it could mean getting burned. The radiator was fueled by oil. Every month in cold weather the Argo Oil truck pulled up in our driveway, and a huge hose was sent through a basement window to pour oil into the furnace. To avoid high heating bills in winter, our thermostat had to be turned down every night and turned up again in the morning, something that is true even today. In the 1930's, however, our thermostat was located in the basement, so that in addition to running down to turn the hot water heater on and off, one of my parents also had to run down to adjust the heat. Eventually, we got a thermostat on the second floor.

Mother did her ironing in the kitchen on Sunday nights, piling the ironed clothing on a white metal table that stood against a wall. In preparation, she had to sprinkle each item of clothing with drops of water and roll it into a ball to dampen for an hour or so. The iron she used was black and heavy.

While Mother ironed, I sat on the floor with my back supported by the narrow archway that divided the kitchen from the breakfast nook and we listened to all the Sunday night comedy shows: Jack Benny, Fibber McGee and Molly, Fred Allen. My little brother had been put to bed and my father was in the living room reading the rest of his Sunday newspapers. It was a time of shared pleasure between my mother and me.

The back hall that led to the basement also had a flight of stairs leading up to an attic. This was a source of mystery and curiosity. I was not allowed to go up there because both the stairway and the attic were filled with dust. Mother did not want all that dirt tracked back into our flat, nor did she want to clean yet another floor. Interesting things were stored there, I was certain, and I wanted to know what they were. My desire to know was intensified after I read a Nancy Drew mystery called *The Secret in the Attic*. I never did find out what was hidden there.

The living room had a fireplace. On cold winter nights Daddy opened the flue, piled in newspapers, wood and charcoal, and I lay on the floor watching the flames shoot upward, studying the colors that changed from blue in the center to red, yellow and orange around the sides. There was a dark green carpet and our furniture was upholstered in dark green and maroon, a popular color combination of the late1930's. Mother had read about it in "Women's Day" and "The Ladies Home Journal." This was the room where Daddy read his newspaper and Mother, her novels. My brother and I were allowed to play in the living room, but with only one toy at a time, so there would be no mess. We had wooden blocks and Lincoln Logs; I had dolls and Dick had toy cars and trucks.

When my brother and I ran or jumped inside the house, the sound reverberated into the flat below. Our parents were constantly saying, "Quiet! There are people downstairs!" We must have heard that exclamation thousands of times.

The living room was also where Daddy's string quartet played once a month, when it was his turn to host. The quartet played music by Mozart, Haydn and Schubert. Unlike the noise my brother and I made running, no neighbor ever complained about the music. If I was very quiet I was allowed to stay in the room and listen.

Just off the living room was a small room called the alcove, which held Mother's piano, a small record player and several bookcases. Mother liked to play and sing romantic popular music, as well as simplified versions of classical themes. Sometimes Daddy accompanied her on his violin, and when I was old enough, I sang along with them, reading the words over Mother's shoulder. When I took lessons on the violin and, more briefly, on the piano, this was the room where I practiced.

From the alcove a door opened onto a porch with a railing and an awning. It held a glider and two metal chairs that bounced. It was in the front of the house, overlooking the street. In summer, this was my favorite place to read. I spent hours lying on the glider, a pile of books on the floor beside me. Sometimes mother set up a bridge table and I could draw or color or play board games with a girlfriend.

From 1937 until 1950, the years we rented the upstairs flat, three or four different families moved in and out downstairs. They were all friendly and had children Dick and I played with. This changed during autumn of my senior year of high school. New owners bought the building and moved into the downstairs flat. Several weeks later they informed my parents that they needed our flat for their relatives. We had no choice: after 13 years in that home, we would have to move out when our lease ended the following summer.

Playmates

∾

"Go out and play," my mother says on weekends, after school, and every morning in the summer. "Get some fresh air."

I change into my play clothes (old blue jeans, tattered gym shoes and a polo shirt), race down the stairs and seek out the kids on the block. I love the freedom of being outdoors.

I have two sets of friends. Grace, Danny and Eric live on my side of the block; in fact Grace lives downstairs. The other set, Suzy and Pearl, live nearby: Suzy across the street and Pearl around the block from Suzy. They are both in my class in school. For some reason, they never seem to play with Grace, Danny and Eric.

Grace is two grades ahead of me, but doesn't mind playing with me. One of the games we play is called Russia, short for Russian hand-ball. We use the side of our house, standing in the narrow driveway as far from the wall as we can get, and toss the ball against the wall, let it bounce and catch it after performing complicated maneuvers involving arms and legs. If you miss, it's the other person's turn. I play this game alone if Grace isn't home. I doubt that the Russians, who, my parents tell me, are far away fighting the Nazis, ever heard of our game.

The winter before I turn ten, I discover Monopoly. Grace owns the only set around, which propels me, daily, down stairs to ask her to play with me. After a few weeks of this, she tires of the game, but I persist. She tries to compromise: "We'll play for one hour, and whoever has the most money, wins," she says. I balk at the time restriction, but it's that or no game. I'm turning into a Monopoly addict.

Grace and I both have brothers named Dick. Her brother is four years older than she; mine is four years younger than I am. Neither of them plays much with us because of the age differences. Grace's brother is a genius in science, and has a chemistry set in the basement of our shared house, where he is always doing experiments. Many of the experiments send an odor like rotten eggs up through the laundry chute into both flats. I don't know what his mother thinks, but my mother is very angry. When he grows up, he becomes a scientist for the Atomic Energy Commission in Washington D.C.

Grace is a tall, heavyset girl who gets the best marks in school. At eleven, she is physically awkward. When she runs up or down our staircase, her heavy oxfords are noisy. This annoys my father, who one day remarks impatiently that she clumps. "Sounds like a cow on the back stairway," he says. I am startled, because I've never heard my father talk unkindly about anyone, and because she is my friend.

Shortly after that, Grace and I get into an argument about who has the most points in our game of Russia. "You can't add," she says, "You're just a baby."

Now I have a trump card. "Oh, yeah?" I retort. "Well, my father says you clump like a cow."

Grace runs inside crying.

My mother gives me a lecture I have always remembered, about never insulting people and never repeating what you hear in the privacy of your own house.

She also sends me downstairs to apologize to Grace.

I don't pester her about Monopoly after that. But we still play together with Danny and Eric.

Danny lives three houses east of us. He's an only child with a strict mother, and is the bossiest kid on the block. One of his jobs is Guardian of the Grass: he makes certain no one steps on a blade of grass on his lawn.

"It kills the grass," he says

All of us run over lawns everywhere on the block and I've never seen one without grass. But we are very careful not to step on his lawn. I think his mother put him up to this.

Whenever there are three of us outside, the group summons the fourth, standing outside the house and calling in sing-song voices, loudly, "Eric, come out and pla-ay." Sometimes at night, in the summer, my friends call for me outside my bedroom window. "Judy, come out and pla-ay." I'm too embarrassed to let them know I'm in my pajamas, having already been put to bed.

"I'll go see if I can come out," I shout down through the open bedroom window. But I know there is no use asking. It's getting dark, about eight o'clock. I wait, pretending, and then, without having left my room, I call back, "I can't. I'll see you tomorrow morning." Then I get back in bed, sulking over my unfair fate of having the earliest bedtime on the block, and the strictest parents.

We never rang doorbells: that might incur the anger of a busy mother, or, in Eric's case, a busy aunt. *Tante* took care of Eric while his parents and his older sister, Dorothy, were at work. *Tante* also did the cleaning and cooking in the house. I never saw his mother, and suspected that maybe he had no real parents. Although I had been in the homes of Grace and Danny, I never was inside Eric's house farther than the back hallway. Peeking inside from there, I could see that the shades were drawn and the rooms were dark. There was a funny smell in the hallway, probably a mixture of cooked cabbage and general mustiness from never being aired out.

Eric was the youngest of our group. His family had come recently from Europe and he spoke to *Tante* in Yiddish, although he also spoke perfect English. Eric had difficulty with the small things in life: he could not tie his shoes or button his knickers. We were always saying, "Button your pants, Eric," or "Your laces are untied."

The four of us played hide and seek, statues, tag, touch football and kick- the-can. If we didn't have a tin can, we used Danny's hat. In statues, the person who was IT took each of us by the arm, swung us around and abruptly let go. We had to stand perfectly motionless in whatever off-balance position we landed, while the IT person decided who the most interesting statue was. The winner then became IT.

My games with Suzy and Pearl were tamer. In summer we sat on someone's front porch and played school or board games or colored. Pearl was content with whatever we decided to do. She was very easy to get along with. Suzy was the leader of the three of us, and the only one who was not Jewish. Her family belonged to the Methodist church on Twelfth Street and West Grand Boulevard. Suzy decided what we would play, and insisted on being the teacher when we played school. She had curly hair, knew how to sew, had beautiful handwriting and strong opinions about everything. She got perfect marks in school. Her father was a long-distance trucker so he was away from home a lot. I liked to play at her house. Even her *parents* went barefoot indoors, something my father would never allow!

In our trio, two of us were often close and the third was left out. When Suzy and I were best friends, we didn't invite Pearl to play. When I tired of Suzy, Pearl and I dressed in the same colors, had sleep-overs and ignored Suzy. Of course, there were also many times when Suzy and Pearl were playing together and didn't include me. Mother explained to me that this is how girls were at ten, and I had to accept that they were only doing the same thing I had done to each of them.

That didn't make me any happier about being left out.

One day when Pearl and I were playing in my bedroom, my mother overheard me telling her something Suzy had told me in confidence. After Pearl left, my mother asked me to please sit down with her in the living room. I felt a sense of foreboding.

"If you tell Pearl a secret about Suzy, Pearl will think you can't keep secrets, and she won't trust you," my mother said. "And then if Pearl tells Suzy what you said about her, Suzy will be mad at you. Anything someone tells you that's private has to stay private. Otherwise you'll lose your friends."

I have always tried to heed this advice. Years later, when I was a psychotherapist, the issue of client confidentiality was particularly easy for me to respect.

It's a hot summer day, shortly after my 10th birthday, and I'm on my downstairs front porch with Suzy. "We're going to play Sunday school," she announces. "And I'll show you how the Jews killed Jesus."

She backs me up against the wall. "See, they put his arms out like this. . ." Suzy takes my arms and presses them, outstretched, against the hot brick wall. I'm too surprised to protest; besides, Suzy is a year older and a head taller than I am. I'm not only surprised about being pushed against the wall; I am surprised at the information. I never heard anything about this at my Sunday school at Temple Beth El.

"And then they put nails in his hands . . ."

At that moment the back of my hand, pushed by hers, presses against the doorbell. Moments later my mother comes running downstairs. She is wearing an apron, and her hair is damp against her forehead. I have a sick feeling in the pit of my stomach, but I don't think I have done anything wrong and I don't know why I feel so scared.

"If you want something, just come upstairs," my mother starts in. "Why do you have to ring the doorbell? I just washed the kitchen floor, and I've been ironing, and I'm hot and tired and . . ."

"Oh, Mrs. Wise, we're sorry," Suzy apologizes. "I was just showing Judy how the Jews killed Jesus."

My mother's face reads as if I killed Jesus myself. I'm not quite sure who Jesus is, but I'm very sure about my mother's anger.

"It wasn't the Jews, it was the Romans," she manages to tell Suzy. "Now you go home for lunch. And you," she says, turning to me, "get upstairs. You can help me fold the laundry."

It is even hotter on the second floor than on the front porch, and the steam coming from my mother's eyes doesn't help. But once I realize she isn't mad at me, or even Suzy, but at Suzy's church, the sick feeling goes away. Finally she finishes ironing and makes us both some ice cold lemonade. Then she goes to her room for a nap and I wander downstairs to see if Grace might, just for once, be the one to suggest a game of Monopoly.

Being Jewish: Grade School

❧

The Purim Party

I stand outside my house on the edge of the lawn near the curb, feeling painfully conspicuous in my long blue dress. When I move around, I trip on the hem. My mother has sewed this dress for me for the Purim party at the Temple Beth El Sunday school. I'm holding a sheaf of wheat; pieces break loose from my bundle and fall in the grass. I'm waiting for a lady to pick me up in her car because my mother doesn't know how to drive. I wish the lady would hurry; I imagine everyone on the block wondering why I'm wearing a costume in April, when it isn't Halloween. If anyone asks me, I don't know how to explain Purim, even though Mother told me the story:

Long, long ago there was a Persian king. His evil advisor, Hamen, told him to kill the Jews. The king's wife, Esther, was an outsider, but she saved everybody. Even though she was scared, she told the king, "If you kill all the Jews you will have to kill me because I'm Jewish, too." The king loved Esther so much that he changed his mind and the Jews were saved.

"All the children will be dressed like characters in the story," my mother told me. "You'll be Esther, a simple country girl before she became the queen." I guess that's why I have the wheat. Anyway, right now no one else is around, so I don't have to explain the story. But they could be looking out of their windows. At last, the lady drives up and I can hide in her car.

The party is in a large room at the Temple and I don't see anyone from my 1st grade Sunday school class. Alone and unhappy, I stand near the doorway clutching my sheaf of wheat, when I hear one woman say to another angrily, "What's this stuff dropping all over the floor?"

I try to blend into the wall, but they spot me, and the other woman says, in a more kindly tone, "We'll just put this bundle over here until you're ready to leave." I want to leave at that very moment, but I'm stuck. I try not to cry. It's one thing for me to hate the bundle of wheat, but quite another for these strangers to take it away from me. My mother gave it to me, and even though I don't want it, I'm scared she'll be upset when she finds out.

A nice lady sees me standing alone and gives me a *hamantashen*, but the triangular pastry is filled with prunes, which I hate, and I don't know where to throw it away. I remain tearfully at the edge of the room, waiting until it is finally time to retrieve the wheat and go home.

At the Edge

For a good part of my life as a Jew, I continued to stand at the edge, not fully an insider, not quite belonging. Everything I recall from my Jewish childhood in the 1930's and '40's came with conflict. Each early encounter being Jewish brought a disliked activity, disharmony in the family, or ostracism from my public school classmates.

My memories are not joyous or filled with a sense of belonging or pride. My parents themselves were conflicted, within themselves and between one another, so how could they transmit to me anything more than that? My mother tried; my father was, at best, indifferent. There was not enough love of being Jewish in my family, then, to compensate for the feeling of not quite belonging.

The upstairs flat we rented for 13 years was at the outer edge of the largest Jewish neighborhood in Detroit. The streets north and west of ours housed a large Jewish population. Our street, however, was mixed, Jewish and Gentile. All the other Jewish kids I met at school lived in the midst of the "Jewish section." Many of their parents, like my grandparents, were born in Europe and went to Orthodox synagogues. My American-born parents had no contact with them.

My parents, especially my father, preferred being in a mixed neighborhood. While he did not deny his Jewish identity, I never saw him show much interest in it. The oldest of six children of Russian immigrants, he grew up in Montana, where there were barely ten Jewish men to form the required *minyan* at his bar mitzvah. In fact, he never told me he'd had a bar mitzvah until my own sons were approaching that age. His reluctance to talk about it suggested to me that he had felt shame at being an outsider, a first-generation Jew whose parents spoke with heavy European accents, amid the farmers and cowboys of the Wild West.

No Christmas Tree

One of the few things I had always loved about being Jewish was getting a present every day for eight days for Hanukkah, instead of just getting one present on Christmas. I thought that was terrific, until my friend Suzy put a different idea in my head.

"Where do you put your presents if you don't have a tree?" she demanded. "You *have* to put them under the tree—that's the best part!"

I so informed my mother, who informed me back that Jews did not have Christmas trees because we did not celebrate Christmas, and that was the end of that. Even the year I learned in school that the Christmas tree tradition began in celebration of the Winter Solstice, she would not discuss it. I enjoyed the eight-night ritual of lighting Chanukah candles, but I always felt deprived because we didn't have a tree.

Jewish Food

If our Jewishness had a category, I would say we were culinary Jews. On Sunday mornings Grandpa Apple, my mother's father, came over with bagels and lox, smoked fish and pickled herring. My mother often made cabbage borscht, stuffed cabbage rolls, *lukshen kugel* (noodle pudding), roast chicken and brisket. We had *hamentashen* with jam for Purim, fried *latkes* (potato pancakes) for Chanukah and a big meal with brisket and potatoes for Rosh Hashanah. Sometimes, as a special treat, we had supper at Boesky's Delicatessen, where we could order potato *latkes*, cheese blintzes and kosher corned beef sandwiches.

I loved going to Grandma Apple's house on Friday nights for chicken noodle soup, boiled chicken and fresh *challah*. Grandma Apple "kept strictly kosher." That meant she bought meat and poultry only from the kosher butcher, had separate sets of dishes and silverware for meat and dairy dishes, and changed over her entire kitchen at Passover. However, my mother's parents did not, so far as I know, ever go to religious services at a synagogue.

My mother had a belief in God and always wanted to do the right thing. She wanted to please her mother by keeping a kosher home. My father, an avowed agnostic, didn't want a kosher kitchen in his home. "That's just a lot of work and foolishness," he proclaimed. While this may have made the physical part of organizing the kitchen easier for her, it put her at odds with her own mother, who refused to come to our house to eat. When Grandpa Apple came to our house on Sunday mornings, Grandma did not come with him. Many Friday nights after Grandpa died, my brother and I walked with Mother to Grandma's for *shabbas* supper. Daddy stayed home.

Mother tried to observe other Jewish traditions, but my father didn't make it easy for her. On Yom Kippur, the Day of Atonement, my mother fasted, while my father prepared his own meals in the kitchen. On Passover, she cleared the house of bread and served matzo in its place. I particularly recall one year when I was about ten. She had cooked for two days to prepare our Sedar, making gefilte fish, chicken soup with matzo balls, chopped liver, roasted chicken and Passover sponge cake.

"Where's the bread?" my father demanded.

"It's Passover. We're having matzoh."

"I want my bread. And put away the Haggadah. I'm not reading any service."

My brother and I glanced at each other across the table. We were silent. My chief memory is of the tension and silence in the room as we ate the carefully prepared meal. I went to bed that night feeling a deep sadness for my mother.

Sunday School

Because my father refused to join a religious congregation when I was very young, my mother sent me to children's services on the High Holidays (Rosh Hashanah and Yom Kippur) with her unmarried sister at Temple Israel, the largest Reform congregation in Detroit. My Aunt Elizabeth loved to show me off to all her friends.

"This is my little niece, Judy," she told them, as I squirmed with discomfort at the attention.

The services were boring and I didn't know any of the other children. The only thing I remotely enjoyed was the deep, dramatic voice of Rabbi Fram, the Senior Rabbi, as he told stories from the pulpit.

When I started first grade, my mother convinced my father to let me go to Sunday school at Temple Beth El, the only other Reform congregation in Detroit, the one where my other aunts and uncles belonged. Evidently I could attend without my parents becoming members. So, during early elementary school I went to Sunday school. I remember little except that I would have preferred to sleep late. By fourth grade I refused to go. Since I had my father on my side, I was able to quit.

The most satisfying thing I recall from my early days at Temple Beth El was memorizing a bedtime prayer. As a little girl, I recited it every night with my mother as she tucked me into bed:

In peace, O God, I shut my eyes,
In peace again I hope to rise.
While I take my nightly rest,
Be with those I love the best.
Guide me in Thy holy way;
Make me better every day.
Shema y'Israel
Adonai Eluhenu
Adonai echud.
Hear, O Israel,
The Lord our God,
The Lord is One.
Amen.

Long after I stopped going to Sunday school, I said the prayer. When I was a child and my grandparents died, my mother assured me they were watching over me, looking down from heaven. Many years later, immersed in a secular humanistic Jewish temple, I was secretly grateful to know my mother had been a believer. It was one of many bright spots in the heritage I received from her.

Long after the *Shema* was dropped from our humanistic liturgy, I began to use it as a mantra when I meditated. I felt deliciously subversive.

Shampooing

☙

Some of the most intimate moments I recall with my mother happened when she was shampooing my thick, dark hair each week. There was a combination of physical closeness, her scalp massage and the stories she told me about her childhood.

I sat on a high chair facing away from the bathroom sink, leaning my head backward against a folded towel perched on the rim, the way women did in the beauty shop. Although I could not see my mother's face, I could sense the warmth of her body as she stood beside me. I felt comforted and secure, even when my neck hurt.

Mother filled the basin with warm water and used a metal measuring cup to pour the water over my head many times, to thoroughly wet my hair. Then she applied a small amount of Ogilvie Sisters Castile Soap Shampoo to the crown of my head, being very careful not to let the liquid spill into my eyes. With her fingertips, she massaged suds into my scalp and over my long hair. I liked the strong, clean odor of the shampoo.

Rinsing was more difficult than washing. The sink was emptied, then again filled with clean warm water, and as much of my head as possible was "dunked" so the soap would rinse out. This took two or three sink-fillings. Then my hair was rinsed once again with warm water from the metal cup, which was filled from the tap. Getting the water the right temperature was complicated by the fact that there were two water taps, hot and cold, so that the two independent streams had to be mixed in the cup carefully.

Sometimes my hair needed two soapings, so this ritual took quite a long time. When my neck began to feel uncomfortable, Mother waited while I shifted my position. After the soap was adequately rinsed out, there was the vinegar rinse: a small amount of vinegar in a bit of warm water. This softened the hair and took out tangles, much as a commercial "tangle-free" rinse does today.

What I liked, besides the extended time with my mother and the feel of her fingertips massaging my scalp, were the stories she shared about her childhood. Most of them involved her older sister and the ways in which she persecuted my mother. In one of my favorite stories, Elizabeth decided she did not want this baby sister any longer. She was in the process of pulling Evelyn by her hair down the long flight of steps from the second story of their house, when their mother caught her. Grandma screamed, picked up the baby, and punished Elizabeth, who had been on her way to dump her sister in the garbage can.

Elizabeth teased my mother endlessly about her red hair. In those days, my mother told me, people with red hair were called "carrot top" and laughed at. Mother was always self-conscious about being "different."

In another story, Elizabeth was walking down that same staircase when her long dark hair grazed the gas lamp on the wall and caught fire. ("Why was there a gas lamp?" I asked. "Because we did not yet have electric lights," my mother explained.) Once again, Grandma came to the rescue, this time wrapping her older daughter's head in a bath towel to smother the flames. Much of Elizabeth's hair and eyebrows were singed away, and it took some time before they grew back.

This story both horrified me and filled me with a sense of justice being done to the girl who tried to do away with my mother and who laughed at her beautiful red hair. "Tell me about Aunt Elizabeth getting her hair burned off," I would beg each time my mother began to wash my hair.

Mother also told me about her mother, Fanny, my Grandma Apple. When Fanny was a girl, back in Russia, she saw someone drown in a lake. She herself could not swim, and the drowning terrorized her. Because of her fear of water, she forbad my mother to go swimming. My mother, however, defied her mother's orders by taking swimming lessons at the local YWCA in Rochester, NY, where she grew up. (This, in itself, shocked me: I thought of my mother as perfect and could not imagine her being disobedient.)

There were other stories about Fanny. At fifteen, she ran away from the *shtetl* (village)where she lived with her family and came alone on a boat to America. Fanny was a dark haired, feisty beauty, and headstrong. She left Russia without saying goodbye to her own mother. For the rest of her life she tried to make up for her guilt. She kept a kosher home, cooked the

26

finest Jewish foods, and sewed all her daughters' clothing herself. All the cooking, sewing and cleaning left her short tempered. She was frequently angry with her husband, a gentle, jovial man who, unfortunately, tended to drink too much and to gamble away his earnings.

I could barely relate to these stories. It was only recalling them in later years that gave me some understanding of my mother. At the time I heard them, they were of a world beyond my imagination. I could not picture my Grandma, a stooped woman with white hair, as a teenager, and certainly not as one who did something as rebellious as to run away from home, cross an ocean and never see her family again. But I loved the stories.

When the rinsing and the stories came to an end, Mother wrapped my head in a large bath towel and helped me sit up. Next, she brushed out any tangles that remained after the vinegar rinse. Then she parted my hair carefully in the middle and formed large, vertical curls, fastening each one with a bobby pin to hold it in place until it dried. (Electric hair dryers, like television and computers, did not yet exist.) My hair retained the curl for several days. As a variation, and especially when the weather was warm, she made a thick braid on either side of my head, leaving a long curled strand at the end.

This way of washing my hair began when I was very small and continued even after I was attending Intermediate School. I think my mother enjoyed telling stories of her childhood as much as I liked hearing them. From my present perspective, I would guess there was something therapeutic, healing, in telling me how things had been, even though (or especially because) they were not happy memories for her. For me, it was special to be the object of my mother's attention for such an extended period of time and not be scolded for anything. I wonder, now, if her mother had done the same for her, washing her hair and telling her stories.

It never occurred to me to ask.

Sick-In-Bed

∽

When I was sick and lay a-bed
I had two pillows at my head
And all my toys beside me lay
To keep me happy all the day

. . .

from "The Land of Counterpane"
in *A Child's Garden of Verses*
by Robert Louis Stevenson

When I am sick, my parents take turns reading to me. The lines above are among my favorites, although I don't relate to the next part, in which the little boy's toy soldiers march up and down the blankets. I don't understand how he could get them to stand up if he moved so much as an inch. Besides, I'm a girl and don't play with toy soldiers.

My blue wool blanket is littered with paper dolls, books, scissors, lined loose-leaf and colored construction paper, and my favorite stuffed animal, a black dog named Scottie, who wears a red plaid ribbon around his neck. Behind my back are two pillows, plumped up to give me extra support. On the table next to the bed, alongside my lamp, is a box of Kleenex, half empty. Near the side of the bed is a blue metal wastebasket, both filled and surrounded by used pieces of Kleenex.

I am the Queen, reigning over my empire. I am officially Sick-in-Bed, with a cold and fever, allowed to stay home from my third grade classes. Mother keeps me camped out beneath the blankets so I won't be tempted to run around, which might deplete my already low energy. Today my fever is lower and I feel well enough to enjoy the privilege of being home for the third day. The first two days all I did was sleep, sneeze and listen to a few of my favorite radio programs. When my fever is very high, mother pats my arms, legs and body with rubbing alcohol to cool me down. I love the soft touch of her hand against my skin.

Mother comes in often to check on me. She takes my temperature, gets me up to go to the bathroom and brings me glasses of water or juice. "It's important to drink a lot of fluids," she reminds me. She fixes my favorite meals: Cream of Wheat with a raisin face for breakfast, chicken noodle soup for lunch, hot chocolate to drink in the afternoon, and something light for supper, perhaps French toast. Normally lamb chops are my favorite meal, but I don't have enough appetite to eat meat this week.

Unlike normal days, when I go to school and then play outside with my friends on the block, being sick means extra loving care from Mother. If I ask nicely, she will read me a story, or take a few minutes from her housework to sit on the edge of the bed and chat with me. She is very firm, however, about not letting me get up. "The doctor said you should stay in bed," she tells me when I complain.

The doctor is God. His name is Joe Himmelhoch. He is short and round, and full of energy and good humor. He comes to the house every day to check on how I am doing. When I was very little, about two or three, I cried every time I heard his footsteps on the stairs. He came into the house singing his theme song:

Last night I saw upon the stair
a funny little man who wasn't there;
he wasn't there again today,
Oh, how I wish he'd go away.

The song is intended to make me laugh, but instead I cry, every time. One day, when I am four, I wonder how it would be if I *don't* cry this time. I can actually picture the doctor coming in singing, and myself not crying. When the doorbell rings, I not only don't cry, I *cannot* cry. There is no fear and no tears. I can't even fake it. This happening surprises me so greatly that I don't even mind the exam that follows.

Dr. Himelhoch enters my bedroom like a small whirlwind, talking and telling jokes the entire time he is with us. He uses a tongue depressor to look down my throat. He looks inside my ears with another instrument and listens to my heartbeat with his stethoscope, pressing it to my chest and then my back. He gives my mother a bottle of red cough medicine for me to take and gives me a lollypop. "When the fever is gone for 24 hours, she can go back to school," he says. Then, singing his "little man upon the stairs" song, he is gone. The house feels emptier.

I turn to the construction paper, to design a cover for a book report I must turn in when I return to school. I also have to write the book report. I have finished reading the book, *The Little Cabin in the Woods*. It, along with several others, is part of the pile on my blanket. In my careful cursive handwriting, I begin the report. When it is completed, I call out to my mother. I want her to read it and also to bring me some crayons so I can do the cover. She comes in looking a bit impatient, but softens when I tell her I want her to read my report and that I need crayons.

"I think if you feel well now, you could make the cover at the table in the breakfast nook," she offers. "And maybe you would like some warm milk with honey to drink."

I put on my slippers and my bathrobe. I am delighted to be able to get out of bed, and I do feel much better. While I am in the kitchen, Mother changes the rumpled sheets on my bed and straightens up the room. At the table in the breakfast nook, I design a cover and use a hole-puncher to make two holes that line up with those on the loose leaf paper of the report. Mother brings some yarn to tie it all together. She has read the paper.

"I think it's very good," she tells me. "Be sure to show it to Daddy when he comes home from the office."

I feel warm and happy inside: the fever is gone, the sneezing has slowed to once an hour, and my work is finished. Mother has been especially nice to me all afternoon. It's raining outside, so I haven't missed any fun outdoors. And perhaps tomorrow I can return to school. Or at least take a bath, put on regular clothes and not have to be in bed.

Measles

The room is darkened. The shades are pulled down, and towels are hung over the edges of the windows, to keep any light from coming into the room. I cannot read; I can scarcely see to eat. Not that I feel much like eating. I feel weak, hot (Mother says I have a high fever) and it is all I can do not to rub the places on my skin that itch so badly. There is no remedy

31

for measles and there is a grave danger: light can damage the eyes, can even lead to blindness.

The hallway outside my bedroom is also kept in the dark with blankets hung over the openings to the dining room and the front hall. The bathroom, too, has a towel hung over the frosted glass window. I have already suffered through chicken pox, another illness with red bumps and itching, but this is many, many times worse. With chicken pox, I didn't have to stay in the dark.

For ten days I stay in my bedroom, except for occasional trips to the bathroom. Much of the time I'm asleep. It is the awake times that are so troublesome. Because measles is highly contagious, no one comes into the room except my parents, to bring me food, water and emotional comfort. But they cannot hug or kiss me. The red spots on my skin could transfer to them. Mother pats my skin with lotion on sterile cotton balls to ease the itching, but it doesn't help much.

Finally, after what seems like a year of days, the red spots begin to dry up, to get smaller and scabby. I don't itch any longer. I don't feel so tired, either. The doctor comes and says that tomorrow it will be safe to be in daylight, and in a few days I can return to school. I feel excited as I think about returning to my normal life.

The towels come down from the windows and the blankets from the hall doorway. I am allowed to take a bath. Mother puts baking soda in the water to soothe my skin. Sitting in the warm bath feels like a brand new experience. I am aware of the difference in temperature between the warm water and the cooler air. I slide down on my back so that as much of my body as possible is beneath the water level. The warmth and wetness of the water sooth me, remind me of mother's hand rubbing lotion on my skin, long ago before the measles.

After the bath I get dressed, read my books and, at long last, sit on the upstairs front porch. I feel the soft breeze on my face, smell the freshness of the spring air, hear birds chirping and allow daylight into my eyes. My friends gather below on the lawn of my house and call up to me.

"Are you done with the measles?" they ask. "When can you come out to play?"

Yes, and *soon*, I tell them. I am still weak from so many days in bed, but I am so happy to be out of the dark bedroom and not itch that I don't even beg to go downstairs.

Helping the War Effort

⌒

It is a little after 7:00 p.m. on a cold winter evening. Mother is in the kitchen, singing as she finishes washing the dinner dishes; Daddy is in the living room behind the newspaper; my little brother is in bed and I am in my pajamas, sitting on the floor in my bedroom, playing jacks and listening to *The Lone Ranger* on my radio. Suddenly a loud wailing sound enters through the closed windows of the house and I hear my parents scurrying to turn out all the lights. The sound is a siren and this is a blackout alert. I turn off my lamp and the radio and move carefully down the dark hallway to the living room.

My father has just put on his overcoat and hat and, with a special, tiny flashlight in hand, dons his Air Raid Warden armband and heads down the stairs from our upper flat to the street. His task is to make certain that all the neighbors have turned out their lights. I try to peer out the window to see if I can spot him walking. I have just enough time to notice the blackness with no streetlamps before mother tugs me away from the draperies and hastily pulls down the window shades.

My parents have previously explained to me that we were only practicing, in case enemy bombers flew overhead, so they could not see where to drop their bombs. Still, it is an eerie feeling to sit with my mother in the darkened living room, whispering and imagining bombs falling. I am very relieved when the "all-clear" siren sounds and we can turn on the lights once again.

I was only eight years old in 1941 when Pearl Harbor was attacked by the Japanese, bringing the United States into World War II. From then until VJ-Day, in August of 1945, consciousness of the war was very much a part of my life. Blackouts were only a part of the picture, but a big part. My father had been too young for duty in World War I, and was too old to be called for World War II. I thought he was very lucky, and was proud of him for being an Air Raid Warden, although always a little nervous when he had to go out into the dark, silent night, alone.

Government posters were everywhere: "Uncle Sam wants YOU," "Buy War Bonds" and "A Slip of the Lip Can Sink a Ship." I didn't understand that slogan until my mother explained that if a soldier knew a military secret and told someone, who told someone else, news could reach the enemy and put many people in danger. I thought about that a lot; I was glad I didn't know any military secrets so that I didn't have to worry about accidentally telling one. It felt like a terrible responsibility.

I only knew one soldier. He was a friend of my parents, married but with no children, and younger than my father. His name was Ted and he was a sergeant. (I knew about rank because I had boy paper dolls with uniforms that bore the insignia of all the ranks in the army, and learned to recognize and name all of them, from Private First Class to Four Star General.) Ted was sent to France; I wrote to him and was thrilled when I received letters back. My mother often told me how worried his wife and friends were. He came home safe and unharmed. I considered him a war hero.

In the Detroit elementary schools, theme songs of the Armed Forces were taught in music class. For several years, at Thirkell Elementary, we practiced these songs to the piano accompaniment of our teacher. Six decades later, I can still sing all the words to "We're the Sea-Bees of the Navy," "The Caissons Go Rolling Along," "The Army Air Corps Song," and "The Marine Corps Hymn."

In art class everyone learned how to knit, so that we could make 12 x12 inch squares of wool yarn. These, presumably, were to be sewn together and made into afghans, to be sent to keep our soldiers warm. Outside of school, adults were encouraged to knit wool socks, also to be sent to the soldiers.

Every week we took our pennies and dimes to school to buy Savings Stamps. The money went for the War Effort. The stamps went into a book, and enough filled books could be turned in for a War Bond. The lowest priced bond cost $18.75, but if you saved it for ten years, you could cash it in for $25.00. That seemed very impressive to me when I was eight. Earning the dimes and pennies ourselves was also part of helping the War Effort. I earned money by shoveling snow in winter and watering the garden in warm weather.

At home in the kitchen, Mother poured melted fat, from bacon or fatty meats or gravy, into a large tin can and put it in the refrigerator to harden. When the can was full, she carried it to the local butcher shop for collection, "for the War Effort." The closest to an off-color joke I ever heard from my very proper mother was, "Goodbye. I'm taking my fat can to the butcher."

There were other collectibles. Mother took care of the newspapers and empty tin cans of tuna fish or Campbell's Tomato Soup. My department was tinfoil, saved from the liners of packaged candy and chewing gum. It was waded up into balls and taken somewhere; I have no idea where. Or why. What did they really do with all those wool squares, cans of fat and wads of tinfoil? If they helped us win the war, I don't know how. But participating kept us all feeling very patriotic.

Patriotism was in fashion during W.W.II. One Fourth of July there was a big neighborhood parade. All the children were to wear red, white and blue, and represent the War Effort in some way. I went as Rosie the Riveter (the generic name given to women who went to work in factories, replacing the men who were off to fight the war), wearing navy blue slacks, a white blouse and a red belt. Because of my self-conscious dislike of wearing costumes, I worried all the time I was parading up and down Woodrow Wilson Avenue that I looked too conspicuous in those patriotic colors.

In summer, we grew a Victory Garden in the backyard. The soil in the heart of Detroit was not the highest quality for farming, but Mother managed to coax out carrots, beets, green beans, radishes and green onions from a rectangular patch of added topsoil along the fence that divided our yard from the neighbor's. It was very exciting to check each day to see if the orange tops of the carrots, just beneath the soil, were larger than the day before. The biggest thrill was to eat what we had grown. Like the knitted squares and the tinfoil, I am not sure how this made a difference in the larger picture, but it felt like we were doing Something Important.

During the war, certain things that were used for the soldiers were not easily available to the rest of us. They had to be rationed. When Mother went to the grocery store, she took her Ration Book. Because certain items such as sugar, meat and canned goods were in short supply, she had to give the grocer a ration coupon along with her money. If she used up her ration coupons for the month, she had to wait until next month to buy that item.

She explained to me that rationing stopped rich people from buying up all the good stuff and not leaving enough for others to have. Even the rich people couldn't spend more than the amount of coupons they had.

Among the items rationed was gasoline. It was considered unpatriotic to drive your car any more than necessary; it was permissible, however, to drive to work or for an emergency, such as going to see the doctor. Going for a summer drive in the countryside was now unpatriotic, and also could cause you to run short of your rationed gasoline allotment.

I very much wanted a two wheeled bike when I was ten, but I was told that all metal needed to be used for tanks and planes. Very few bicycles were being manufactured and those in the stores were very expensive. I learned how to ride by borrowing the bike of my neighbor Danny, and did not have one of my own until 1945, when I was twelve and the war was over.

I did not understand too clearly what the war was about, except that a bad guy named Hitler was killing a lot of people all over Europe, and that the United States sent soldiers to help stop his army. Besides Hitler, we were at war with the Japanese, who had bombed us for no reason at all. There were lots of movies about the war that showed airplanes dropping bombs and men on the ground shooting each other with rifles. When I thought about the war at night, lying safely in my bed, I decided that if I were a soldier, I would learn to fly a plane. It seemed safer to be up above dropping the bombs instead of on the ground getting hit by them. I was glad I was a girl, because girls did not have to be drafted into the army.

The movies and some comic strips showed the Japanese as small men with pilot's helmets and big teeth. Americans referred to them, in the movies and sometimes in real life, as "thosedirtyJaps," as though it were all one word. A big part of my early indoctrination was learning to hate them, people whom I had never met, who had bombed our ships and harbor. They, like the Germans, were the Bad Guys. When we ended the war by incinerating them with two atomic bombs, I, innocent, ignorant, and twelve, joined the nation in cheering.

On VJ Day, the day we officially Won the War, I was with my parents and their friends at a vacation spot on Lake Huron. We drove into the nearest town, Lexington. (Unknown to me until many years later, a boy named Bob, two years older than myself, was in that same town celebrating. He was staying at his uncle's cottage: this was the boy/man I would one day marry.) Meanwhile, he and I, separately, joined the gathering on Main Street, where a band played and hundreds joined in a circle dance, spiraling in, out and around, singing, shouting, laughing and crying, all part of something much larger than any one of us alone; a crowd that was proud, patriotic, transported by Victory in a war we never knew first hand, feeling invincible, believing unquestionably in honor, goodness and the moral superiority of the United States of America.

Music in the Air

❦

Growing up in Detroit in the 1930s and '40s, our home was seldom without music. There was an eclectic mix. Mother sang sad love songs ("Falling in Love with Love," "You Forgot to Remember," "Deep Purple") while she cooked or dusted the furniture. Daddy practiced his violin, playing melodies with no words. On Saturday afternoon, *The Metropolitan Opera of the Air*, "*brought to you by Texaco at the sign of the flying red horse,*" played on the radio. Saturday night we listened to *Your Hit Parade,* a half hour of the ten most popular songs of the week.

The same hit songs often remained popular for weeks, even months, moving up or down in their top ten ratings, but affording ample opportunity to be memorized. I learned songs then for which I still remember all the lyrics. My father was not at all interested in popular music; I listened to the *Hit Parade* either with my mother or with my Aunt Mary, my father's youngest sister, who was our babysitter if my parents went out for the evening.

My love of classical music was nurtured very early. When I was four, my father began to take me on Saturday mornings to Orchestra Hall to hear the Detroit Symphony Orchestra children's concerts. Later, when I was in elementary school, I went to the concerts with my mother and my little brother, along with my mother's friend Molly and her daughter, who was close to my age. On Sunday evening at 6:00, all activity halted while my family listened to a classical concert on *The Ford Sunday Evening Hour,* introduced by the initial theme from the 4th movement of the Brahms First Symphony.

From the time I was four, I wanted to play the violin like Daddy. At seven, my wish was granted. Thirkell Elementary School had a music program that gave instruction during school hours. For this privilege, we were allowed to leave our boring geography lesson, making the experience doubly good. The age for beginning lessons was supposed to be eight, but because I was already in third grade at seven, having skipped half of kindergarten and half of 2nd grade, and probably because my father was charming and persuasive, I was allowed into the class. The first violin I played belonged to the school, but before long my father bought me one of my own, half the size of his.

The teacher for the string instruments was Dorothy Romaine, a short, intense woman with very black hair, somewhat older than my mother. Mrs. Romaine taught me to read music, hold the bow correctly and how to care for the violin. Her approach to teaching was very serious. The string class was held in a room with straight-backed chairs, music stands and no desks. There was a blackboard, a lot of chalk dust, and a bare wooden floor. In addition to the eight or ten violinists, there were two cellists and one viola player, a motley group of would-be musicians. Each of us took a turn playing our lesson as a solo, with frequent corrections from Mrs. Romaine, and then we played together, ensemble style. Mrs. Romaine was famous among the children because she tended to spit and spray when she spoke. After class, all of us checked with each other to find out who "got it" that day.

My parents insisted I practice the violin for an hour a day. They began with a half-hour when I was seven, but it soon increased. This was standard when I was a child: everyone I knew had to practice for an hour. My father told stories of being hit with his father's belt if he cut his hour short as a young boy. I was never punished, but I found many ways to stall during practice. *I want a drink of water. I'm hungry. I have to go to the bathroom. Could I go outside now and finish later?* My parents held firm.

I don't know if I had any talent for the violin. My father, not satisfied with Mrs. Romaine, decided to teach me himself. He had begun studying at the age of five, studied all through college, and now played in a string quartet. After graduating from the University of Michigan in the late 1920's, he had been the esteemed Music Critic for the Detroit Free Press, reviewing all the major concerts and soloists who played in Detroit. Why would he hire a teacher?

My father was a perfectionist. He was continually retuning my instrument, readjusting the tension on the bow, informing me when a note was out of tune, telling me a better way to move my wrist and my bowing arm. I don't remember much encouragement from him, just corrections.

Although his comments, which mixed love with impatience, were never harsh, I did not view myself as a very good player. On rare occasions, if the music in my book was written for student and teacher duets, he played along with me, an activity I loved but which he seemed eager to conclude.

There was one issue on which we disagreed when I was young and with which I still disagree, to this day. That was the question of letting me move ahead in my musical learning even when what I was doing was not perfect. There were two instances of this: learning to play 2nd and 3rd positions and using vibrato. My father believed that until I could do 1st position perfectly, there was no point in teaching me either the note-reading or the fingering for 2nd and 3rd positions, which involve higher octaves and an alteration in the position of the left hand. In his estimation, I was not yet ready for the more difficult music that used these notes. As a result, despite having played the violin for six years, from third through ninth grades, I am musically illiterate when it comes to reading anything but the simplest pieces. When, as an adult, I considered taking up the violin again, I could not read the music I wanted to play, and my ability to learn and remember new notes had greatly diminished.

Vibrato was a smaller issue, but came from the same reasoning: if I could not play the notes perfectly in tune, all the time, then what was the use of learning to do vibrato? The result of that omission was to be the only child in the Hutchins Intermediate School Orchestra who played a string instrument without that subtle hand movement that created pulsations in the pitch of each note. This lack was a source of embarrassment to me; I was not the worst player, but close to it. When I entered Cass Technical High school, I was so intimidated by the excellent students in the music department that I simply stopped playing.

If my father did not love listening to me play the violin – which I understand: what young child can play without squeaking on the strings? – I loved listening to him. He played both with a musical score and without, often improvising. He loved to play Fritz Chrysler sonatas, or to practice his part for the monthly string quartet, which was one of the joys of his life. Two were members of the Detroit Symphony and the third was a close family friend. My father sometimes played viola as well as violin parts. The quartet alternated houses each month, and I was ecstatic when it was our turn.

When the quartet played at our upstairs flat on Virginia Park, our living room, which normally had not one item out of place, became strewn with instrument cases, men's jackets and sheet music by Mozart, Schubert and Brahms, dropped carelessly as the group went from one piece to another. I marveled that grown-ups could make a mess and no one said anything about it.

My parents allowed me to stay up later than usual, right in the living room where the quartet was playing, as long as I was quiet. I curled up in the big armchair, watching the way the bow moved across the cello, enjoying the deep tones of the viola, trying to hear my father's notes separately from the blend with the others, enjoying how one of the group stopped everyone in the middle of a line of music to say, "Let's go back to the start of this section; something is off."

Mother loved music as well. She had studied piano since she was a young teen. Her aspirations were less lofty than my father's; she played mainly for her own enjoyment. I have no measure with which to assess her talent, but I don't recall my father ever criticizing her playing, and she seemed able to sight-read every piece she wanted to with no difficulties that I could discern. She preferred playing popular songs to the classics, had many piano books of traditional favorites such as "Comin' through the Rye" and "I'm Always Chasing Rainbows" and often bought sheet music of the latest popular hits. Together we sang the lyrics to "Marzey Doats" and "Chattanooga Choo-choo" and other songs from *Your Hit Parade*.

Sometimes my father joined us, playing the melody line on his violin. I enjoyed this time with my parents beyond words, but toward the end of each session I often spoiled the mood. After several songs my father was ready to stop and move on to other activities, while I begged, "Just one more, can't we do just one more song?"

Mother closed the piano book. Daddy wiped off his violin with a silk handkerchief, loosened the tension on the bow, and placed both in their case, saying, "That's enough! We'll do this again another time if you behave." And Mother added firmly, "I think it's time for you to get ready for bed."

I made a show of stalking off grumpily to my room, feeling the unfairness of a life where the grown-ups got to make all the decisions. But once in bed, after my parents kissed me goodnight, I fell asleep with words and melodies swirling happily inside.

Piano Lessons

For a brief time, when I was about nine, I took piano lessons. If I practiced the piano, I didn't have to practice the violin. My teacher was an elderly man, kind but dull. I did not look forward to my lessons with much enthusiasm. Reading and playing the treble clef was easy for me but when it came to the bass clef, I was always translating: *If this would be middle C for the right hand then it must be two notes lower* and I would hit the A. This method only worked for me if the hands were separate, as in the very beginning lessons. I also had difficulty with rhythm: if both lines were in unison, I could play them together, but if one had eighth notes when the other had half notes, I was in trouble. (I had the same difficulty coordinating my arms and legs properly while learning to swim, although I did not relate this to the piano issue until I was an adult.)

The piano music I recall had simplified classical themes with simplistic lyrics. In this way, I learned to recognize various great works. To this day, when I hear the opening theme of Dvorak's New World Symphony, someone in my head sings *Summer days, lazy days, free of toil and care . . .*

I did not last long at the piano. By the time I started Intermediate School, at eleven, I had given it up. A few years later, however, having stopped playing the violin, I thought it might be fun to take piano lessons once again, perhaps with an older student who was advanced in his or her own playing. There were many such students in my high school music department. Some of them even studied with Mischa Kottler, a renowned Detroit artist whose playing was of national stature and who often soloed with the Detroit Symphony when it reorganized after World War II.

Mr. Kottler happened to have been a friend of my father, and at one time was our next door neighbor, before my brother was born. The moment I expressed an interest in taking lessons, my father phoned this esteemed teacher for a teaching recommendation.

"Oh, I will be happy to teach her myself," said the famous Mischa Kottler. "And Herman, there is no charge. It will be my pleasure."

Anything that had no charge was a big YES in my household. My father accepted the offer, and made arrangements for me to take lessons on Wednesdays at 7:00 pm. I had a feeling deep inside that this was a mistake, but my feelings bore little weight with my parents, who were very excited at this wonderful opportunity for me.

When I arrived at Mischa Kottler's house for my first lesson, the student ahead of me was leaving. I recognized him; he was in the music department at Cass Tech. His name was Emile and he was a very advanced player.

"Hi," he said, "I didn't know you were a music student, too!"

I felt uneasy and out of place, an imposter. "I'm not exactly," I blurted. "Mr. Kottler is a friend of my father and . . ."

At that moment Mr. Kottler appeared and ushered me inside. He motioned for me to sit down at the piano and to choose a piece that I could play from the book he had told my father to buy for me. I chose a simple piece by Bach which I had been practicing for this very moment. But I was so nervous that I kept hitting the wrong keys, which only increased my embarrassment.

Mr. Kottler was very kind and continued to instruct me, but after a few agonizing months, during which time I could not bear the anxiety I felt when I sat at his piano unable to show any progress, I took pity on both of us, and terminated my career in piano.

Summer: Age Ten

❧

The summer I was ten and my brother was six, our family was invited to be the houseguests of my parents' friends, Sigrid and Ob Ruby. They rented a large house every summer in Frankfort, Michigan, three short blocks from a wide expanse of beach on Lake Michigan. The house had an extra bedroom for my parents. Their daughter, Nancy, five years old, shared her room with me, and their son, Carl, shared his with my brother, Dick.

I knew that Mother was uncomfortable about having us be guests for two weeks. My family couldn't afford to rent our own place and had no way to reciprocate, and this was a source of embarrassment for her. She tried very hard not to have our family of four be a burden to her friend: she made our beds, helped prepare meals and clean up, and kept us quiet so we would not annoy the grown-ups. This seemed unnecessary to me, since the Ruby kids were seldom quiet.

The two fathers were also noisy. They played a Rumanian card game called Klobriosh. When one of them had the right combination of cards he would slam them on the table and shout, in a very loud voice, *"Schmeiss!"* They would wake me up several times a night, *schmeising*. "Quiet, Herman, you'll wake the children," my mother would say, but my father was not the loudest one.

Unlike my mother, I didn't mind being a guest at all. The Ruby family welcomed us. I liked their children, even though Carl was still a little kid, two years younger than I was. He was handsome and funny, and did wonderful imitations of Al Jolson singing "Mammy." Although he was only eight and I was ten, I enjoyed him as a playmate. We went to the beach playground by ourselves and he told me stories. He told me how his mother used to take him to the ladies room with her when they were out shopping, and he would peek under the lavatory doors hoping to look up some lady's dress. I was fascinated.

I was also awed by his little sister, who would jump 20 feet off the end of the Frankfort pier into water over her head and swim back to shore. Their mother, Sigrid, tall, blonde and Norwegian, swam every single day of the summer, whatever the weather, in the icy waters of Lake Michigan.

The beach at Frankfort extended perhaps 200 yards east beyond the shoreline, and then narrowed and stretched for what seemed like miles to the north. A long pier acted as a breakwater. The sand was white and fine near the top of the beach, and damp enough to make sandcastles closer to the shore. On the south side of the pier was a playground with swings and slides. Carl could climb up the tall metal poles of the swing- set frame, all the way to the top. He also could swing so high, standing on the seat of the swing, that I was afraid he would flip over the top. His sister hung by the crook of her knees from the climbing bars, the way I had seen kids do on the school playground. These feats intrigued and frightened me; I would never try them myself. I knew Carl's mother thought my mother was over-protective, and I agreed, but this time I was secretly glad.

My mother gracefully swam the breast stroke, keeping her face and hair out of the water. She tucked her long red hair into a rubber bathing cap, and only went to the beach after 4:00 p.m., when the sun was lower and her fair skin would not burn or freckle. She taught me to walk out into the lake, then turn and swim toward shore. My swimming was mostly a dog-paddle. Putting my face in the water hurt my eyes and made me sneeze. Even so, I loved being in the lake.

I was happy during the two weeks we spent in Frankfort. The town was tiny: only three parallel streets wide, most of them with houses. Main Street had a grocery store, a drugstore, an ice cream parlor and a movie theater. Our days had a lazy rhythm. We slept until mid-morning, put on our swimsuits and ate breakfast. Then I would go to the beach with Dick, Carl and Nancy and their mother. We built sand castles and ran in and out of the water, having contests to see who could stay in the cold water the longest. Dick and I watched Carl and Nancy jump off the pier and swim to shore. It was like watching pros in an athletic event: Dick and I did not even think of competing.

My father disliked both sand and immersion in Lake Michigan, and preferred to stay at the house and read. My mother arrived late in the day, after the household chores were done, wearing long sleeves and a hat to protect her from the sun and carrying a novel. Sometimes in the late afternoon we took long walks together. Those were among my closest, most treasured times with her. She pointed out stones and shells, and taught me how to skip a flat stone across the water. She was her freest, most relaxed self at a beach, despite her restrictions about sun and water dangers, and least apt to be critical of my behavior at those times.

About five o'clock we would leave the beach, walk home, bathe off the sand and dress for dinner in blue jeans and T-shirts, fresh socks and saddle shoes. The evenings were comfortably cool. Mother and Sigrid prepared the evening meal and all of us ate together around the large kitchen table. After dinner, perhaps we would walk to Main Street for an ice cream cone, or play a game of Monopoly in the living room, or watch Carl perform an Al Jolson imitation. By 9:30 the children would be in bed, listening to the sounds of adult voices drifting up from the rooms downstairs. Sometimes I read by flashlight, long after we were all supposed to be asleep. Although the radio had reports about our American troops fighting in the War, it could have been on another planet for all it affected us that summer. It was the best two week vacation I'd ever had.

Visiting Chicago

❦

It's the summer before Intermediate School. I'm eleven and have never been away from my family. Aunt Leone, my father's younger sister, invites me to spend a couple of weeks with her family, in Chicago. To my surprise, my parents agree, which challenges my perception that they say "No" to anything that is fun or done without them. My parents drive me to Chicago, a trip of over eight hours. After many admonitions from Mother to be good, take baths, obey my aunt and uncle, write home and have fun, they finally leave.

Aunt Leone, younger than my father by ten years, is married to Morris Alexander, a man who, at that time, had made a lot of money. My parents and other aunts and uncles consider them the "rich relatives." They have three little girls: Lynn, six; Sharon, four; and Joanie, who has her first birthday that summer. (A fourth sister, Diane, is born two years later.) They live on the middle floor of a large, three-family flat, which they do not rent, but own. Actually, they own the entire building, all three floors. The flat is very long from front to back, much bigger than ours. It's on South Shore Drive, a well-trafficked street lined with substantial residential buildings on one side and trees and grass on the other. A block and a half to the right is 71st Street, a busy commercial road where I am not allowed to walk alone.

My first taste of freedom begins when my parents leave. Aunt Leone gives me a lot of responsibility for Joanie, the baby. Perhaps because I am older than her daughters, I seem capable. She allows me to get Joanie out of her crib in the morning. She shows me how to fold and change a cloth diaper; how to insert the large safety pin carefully so it won't stick the baby's tender skin. She points out where Joanie's clothing is kept. After that, I am on my own. I get to change and dress her, like taking care of a live doll.

Aunt Leone shows me how to fix a soft-boiled egg for Joanie's breakfast. She shows me where the bibs are kept, and the washcloth for wiping her face after she's done.

After I lift Joanie from her crib and change her diaper, I put her in the high chair, cook the egg, scoop it out of the shell and feed it to her. I am in seventh heaven. I have never before been given such adult responsibility, and I love the feeling of caring for someone instead of having someone take care of me.

I'm in love with this baby. Her hair falls in dark curly ringlets all over her head. She has wide blue eyes and the long, dark eyelashes that are a trademark of my father's side of the family. She is very responsive and smiles when she sees me. She allows me to care for her without fussing.

After breakfast, the best of all: I carry her down the back stairway to the ground floor, where her stroller is kept, put her into the stroller, and we go for a walk down South Shore Drive. The only crossings are small side streets heading onto South Shore Drive. There are very few cars and I am careful to look both ways. The feeling of freedom, of walking down this street in a city that is not my own, of being in charge of the well-being of this beautiful child, of not having an adult over my shoulder telling me what to do and how to do it: all of this is new and exhilarating.

After our walk, I carry Joanie up the steps and we re-enter the flat. By now the entire family is awake. Aunt Leone is in the kitchen in her robe making pancakes and Lynn and Sharon seem happy to see me. Lynn is reading and Sharon is coloring pictures. Uncle Morrie is dressed to go downtown to work. He comes to breakfast in a dark suit with a white shirt and necktie. He booms questions at me: *How was the walk? Did Joanie behave? Were you careful crossing the streets? Would your parents have let you do this?* I know that he is checking up on me, but I like the attention from him. I feel a loving interest along with his harsh voice. I am also surprised that he seems to know my parents would think I was too young for so much responsibility and pleased that he and Aunt Leone don't agree with them. In my world, my parents' opinions are law. Here, Uncle Morrie is the law.

Which court has jurisdiction is a question that arises on the first night of my visit, at dinner in the formal dining room. We are seated around a long rectangular table, Uncle Morrie at the end to my right and

52

Aunt Leone at the other end. Joan, in her high chair, is next to me, and Lynn and Sharon across from us. The table is set without water glasses for the children. I always have a glass of water with my dinner, and ask if I may please have one. I think this has been a mistake, an overlooked item. I am shocked when Uncle Morrie says *No. Water fills you up and then you can't eat your meal.* His children don't get water with dinner and I don't either.

I argue. *My parents always give me water; I'm thirsty and can't eat unless I have some water to drink.* Uncle Morrie is adamant. I try not to cry. I want the water and I don't like being subjected to his rules. He holds firm. After dinner, I ask if I may please call my parents. Of course I may. I tell them about taking care of Joanie and how much fun I am having. *But Daddy*, I say tearfully, *Uncle Morrie won't let me have any water with my dinner. I want a glass of water when I eat, Daddy.*

My father and Morrie speak with one another. The next night there is water at my place at the table. There is none for Lynn and Sharon, however. He is their father, and he makes the rules for his family.

Uncle Morrie exhibited a sort of power at the dinner table that scared me: I did not want to be the target of it. He picked on the females in his little harem. One at a time, one per meal, he reduced someone to tears. Lynn was spunky and argued with him, but lost. Once he spoke sharply and glared at Joanie, who was smiling in her high chair, until her chin began to quiver, but she kept herself from crying, a feat of self-control that amazed me. Sharon was the quiet, shy one of the family, and he tended to ignore her, which I thought was worse. The night that truly shocked me, however, was the night he yelled at Aunt Leone until she fled the table in tears. I stared into my food and concentrated on eating my mashed potatoes. I was embarrassed for my aunt, uneasy at being a witness to her humiliation, and frightened of Uncle Morrie's angry tongue. After she left the room, my cousins and I finished our meal quickly with no conversation, and asked to be excused from the table.

I had never seen such a thing in my home. In keeping with "children should not be told anything they can tell the neighbors," my parents argued only behind closed doors. Or perhaps they never discussed anything of importance. If they did, it certainly was not in front of Dick and me.

One Sunday, Uncle Morrie took Lynn, Sharon and me to a large amusement park. He bought four tickets for a huge roller coaster called the Silver Streak. I had never been on a roller coaster. I was scared and excited, in equal parts. The seats held three people. Uncle Morrie sat down with his two daughters, one on either side of him. I was in the seat ahead of them.

"I'm scared to go alone," I told him.

"You won't be alone; this man will sit with you." "This man" was a worker at the park. "I'm Jim," he told me.

The roller coaster climbed. And climbed. It went along evenly for a few feet. Then it climbed some more and suddenly we were hurtling downward. I thought my stomach had fallen out. I clung to Jim and screamed. Then it was over. We went along smoothly, until. . . more climbing, more plunging, and nausea set in. "I want to get off!" I screamed back to Uncle Morrie, who was paying no attention. And so it continued until the horrible end. I nearly strangled Jim in my terror and sickness. But I didn't throw up.

When we finally disembarked, my knees were shaking. "You look white as a ghost," Uncle Morrie laughed at me. "Look—your little cousins loved it!" That fact was beyond my comprehension, then and now. I felt weak and nauseous for another two or three hours and have never been on a roller coaster since.

One morning I awoke to the sounds of Lynn in a screaming fight with her mother, who had her by the arm and was leading her toward the bathtub. "Well, we're going and you are coming with!" Aunt Leone said firmly. I noted that "coming with" (or "going with") having no pronoun at the end of the phrase, seemed to be a Chicago way of speaking. "What's wrong?" I asked as we passed in the hallway.

"Oh, Lynnie is so high-strung!" Aunt Leone said in a tone of disgust. I made a mental note to find out later what "high-strung" meant; it did not seem like the right moment to ask.

"She wants me to go clothes shopping with her and I hate it!" Lynn said tearfully before she disappeared behind the bathroom door.

After the baths and the hair brushing and getting dressed "nicely, like ladies," the four of us set out for a little dress shop for children where Aunt Leone bought her daughters several dresses each for school. (Joanie, the baby, was home with a maid.) This kind of shopping expedition was new to me. My clothes were purchased at a discount in New York by my Aunt Elizabeth the Buyer. Other items were purchased for me by a family friend, Ted Schatz, also a children's wear buyer in New York, or by my mother, without me accompanying her.

Here, the saleslady brought out dress after dress. Those that interested someone were kept to try on in the fitting room. Sharon was very compliant and perhaps enjoyed the outing, but Lynn hated every moment. "Just pick something and let's go," she told her mother. But Aunt Leone insisted that she try on each item before they decided.

What surprised me the most, however, was that each girl got four or five dresses, not just one. In my family, the Depression and the War made frugality a way of life. Had I ever gone on such a shopping expedition in Detroit, I undoubtedly would have been allowed to pick just one dress. Never had I seen my mother buy in such quantity as Aunt Leone was doing. I commented on this, and she explained that it was easier for her to pick everything at one time. "Uncle Morrie has a lot of money," she assured me.

Looking back, I had no envy or desire to have a dress of my own; I was simply astonished and fascinated at seeing how different their lives were from mine. Although I didn't know it at the time, the entire visit was my introduction to Comparative Anthropology.

Although I had expected to stay only a couple of weeks, everyone liked having me there and Aunt Leone asked my father to let me stay longer. I was very excited. The visit grew to six weeks. When my parents finally came for me, I was happy to see them, but unhappy that I had to leave this house where I was given freedom, responsibility and trust, as if I were capable. I would miss my friendship with Lynn, whose quick mind devised questions that amazed me and which I could never answer. I would miss the unbelievable sweetness and patience of Sharon, who could string beads for hours, and if they spilled, would begin again without complaint. But most of all, I would miss Joanie. She had become *my* baby. All my young needs for closeness and affection were poured into caring for her, along with a budding maternal love for this beautiful, smiling child. I had never had a pet, but, as I was leaving, I imagined this is how a child might feel if her beloved puppy were taken away.

Aunt Leone had recently taken studio photos of Joanie, her first-year baby pictures. She gave me several of the proofs to take home. I kept them in my bedroom and every night for months, when I went to bed, I looked at the face of that sweet, beautiful child and felt warm tears roll down my cheeks.

The Facts of Life

᪥

One morning after Mother came home from the hospital with my baby brother, she was lying in her bed while he slept in his crib. The window shades were still pulled down, making the room dark. Her bed was very high, but I crawled up beside her, and asked the question that had been burning in my four-year-old mind: "Mommy, how did the baby get out of your tummy?"

"The doctor opened a little door and took the baby out," she told me.

"Where is the door? Can I see it?"

"It's in my side," she said. "But it's only there when it's time for the baby to be born. You can't see it any longer."

This was my earliest piece of sexual misinformation.

Years later, I guessed that she was trying to describe a Cesarean section, although, to my knowledge, she did not have one. My mother was a woman of extreme modesty, which is to say, discomfort about all conversation concerning the human body. It was more than she could cope with to explain vaginal delivery to a four-year-old.

At the age of eight, I was given information by Eric, one of my regular playmates, which was so bizarre that I decided that he had just made it up. It had to do with a song that was popular at the time, "Drinkin' Rum and Coca-Cola." The next lines of the lyrics, which were even played regularly on *Your Hit Parade*, went like this:

....

Go down Point Koomahnah
Both mother and daughter
Workin' for the Yankee dollah

"I can tell you what that means," Eric said with a great air of superiority. It was a Saturday in May, and he had come over to play in our backyard. We were sitting in the grass.

"What it means?" I asked blankly. It had never occurred to me that it meant anything. They were just words with a funny accent and a certain rhythm.

After Eric told me, in explicit detail, what that work consisted of, I informed him he was nuts and should go home. I went into the house and did not tell my mother. I forgot about this conversation for several years. By the time it came back to me, I realized he had not been nuts.

When I was ten, my mother learned from our neighbor that her daughter had started her first period at eleven. The average age for this to happen, in my generation, was thirteen. Mother decided it was time to reveal this secret of womanhood to me, lest I wake up one morning with blood on my sheets and have no idea why. She called me into her room, saying, "Honey, come in here a moment. There is something I want to tell you." I don't know how I knew that whatever it was made her very uncomfortable, but I knew, I sensed it, and I was very gentle with her.

We were in my mother's bedroom. I sat cross- legged on the white chenille bedspread on the double bed my parents shared and Mother sat, facing me, on the bench to her dressing table. I could see the back of her head and my own face in the mirror. I was surprised that she did not mind my sitting on the bedspread, but since it was summer and I had removed my sandals first, I guessed it was okay. More than that, I knew that what she was going to say was more important than the possibility of messing up the neatly made bed.

Mother looked at me very tenderly, so I knew I had not done something wrong; I was not here to be reprimanded. She explained that as a girl approached her teenage years her body went through changes. When that happened, once a month blood came out, for a few days, from a place between her legs. It didn't hurt, she assured me. She showed me what a Kotex pad was, and how to attach it to an elastic belt.

I felt I was being given very serious, adult information. I was pleased that my mother regarded me as old enough to know about this secret.

What my mother was too uncomfortable to tell me was the reason why menstruation occurs, the reason connected to pregnancy and babies. It was another year before I found out that part of the secret.

The following summer, when I was visiting my Aunt Leone and her family in Chicago, a large headline in the Chicago Tribune caught my attention. It was a big story on the front page, and the newspaper was lying right on the breakfast table. The story was something about an unwed mother. It was clear from the story that this woman was in trouble for having a baby, but I did not understand the logic: if a baby were to grow inside of her, I reasoned, why was she blamed for being bad? I thought it was like getting a sore throat or chicken pox: you couldn't help what your body decided to do. I asked my aunt to explain to me why people were so mad at this woman for having a baby grow inside of her.

My aunt looked at me in utter astonishment. "Hasn't your mother ever told you the Facts of Life?" she asked.

"The *what*?" I replied.

"She never told you about menstruation and babies?"

"Oh, yes, she told me about getting a period," I said quickly, eager to defend my mother. "But she never told me about babies."

"Well," said my aunt, "I'm going to give you a book to read. I bought it for Lynn, and I think you should read it." Lynn was only six then; I was puzzled and a little jealous that she already knew something that no one had told me. I also knew that even though Lynn was five years younger than I was, she was incredibly smart, probably already smarter than I was.

The book was called *Being Born*. I read it incredulously, and then reread it. I understood why my mother, bashful as she was about explaining periods, had been unable to tell me the rest of the information, including the part about how my brother really got out.

The top flat in the house my aunt and uncle owned was rented to a family with a girl who was ten, Ruthie. I couldn't wait to share my new information with Ruthie. But there was something that puzzled both of us, and I could not find the answer in the book. The question we had was: Did the father plant a seed in the mother every time they wanted a new baby, or did he just do it once, with the babies coming when they were ready to?

I cast my vote on the side of repeated plantings. Ruthie, however, was positive that they only did it once. She based her belief on what seemed to be empirical evidence.

"My parents' bedroom is right next to mine," she said. "I can even hear them talking. I'm sure if they did *that* before my brother was born, I would have heard them."

Since my parents slept at the farthest end of the long hallway from my room, I had no clue whether she was right.

When I returned to Detroit six weeks later, older and wiser, I told my mother about the conversation with Aunt Leone, and the book I had read. We were in the kitchen; she was washing the dinner dishes and I was drying them. That was always a good time for conversation. When I told her about the book, I could see that she was relieved. Then, with difficulty, because I did not want to embarrass her, I asked the question that Ruthie and I had been pondering all summer. I had almost come to accept Ruthie's theory, but I was not completely convinced. So it was with some surprise that I heard my mother's answer and knew for sure that my parents had actually done it not once, but *twice.*

That fall I started Intermediate School. There were many courses in the curriculum but the one I remember most vividly was the girls' 'seminar' in Sex Education that took place in the balcony of the gymnasium. Those of us who were not playing basketball or volleyball that day, either because we were not chosen or because of reporting "regular", a code word for menstruating, climbed a stairway to the balcony. There were benches against the wall, from which we were supposed to watch our classmates waving their arms in front of each others' faces, trying to get hold of a large ball and throw it somewhere to score a point. I found this totally boring. No one else seemed interested, either.

The balcony conversations provided many bits of sexual information and misinformation over the next three years. There were a number of sources: first, there were the endless "dirty jokes," mostly of the farmer's daughter/traveling salesman variety. In addition to the jokes, there was word-of-mouth information, usually about other people in our class and what they had done with one another and with what amount of clothing on or off. The girls in the balcony either had no stories of their own to report, or they weren't telling. The girls about whom the stories were told were always on the gym floor, waving their arms in the faces of the other team or dribbling up to the basket and sinking the ball through the hoop.

There was also written material. Sometimes it was the "dirty parts" copied out of a book such as *Forever Amber* or *Studs Lonigan* and then passed around surreptitiously, so the teacher would not see it. Sometimes it was a typewritten story by some anonymous author, relating a supposedly true encounter of the sexual kind.

Occasionally there were reports of information I had not read in *Being Born*. If it was not in that book, I usually doubted its veracity, although the other girls discounted my knowledge. In fact, they often told a joke until just before the end and then whispered the punch line because "Judy is too young for this." I was the last one to get to read the printed material, for the same reason. One report, delivered with absolute surety by a chubby girl named Beverly, was that not only men ejaculated. Women did, too.

"I don't think so," I said. "There was nothing about that in *Being Born*."

"That's a dumb book," Beverly said. "I wouldn't even bother reading it."

I tried doing my own research. I had discovered that behind the row of novels on the bookcase in our front hall, there was a second row, well hidden at the back of each shelf. Some of the books were novels and some were more on the order of marriage manuals. When my father was at the office and my mother was taking a nap, or in the basement doing laundry, I snuck out these hidden volumes and devoured all the information about sexual mysteries that I could digest, hastily replacing the books when I heard footsteps that meant my mother was returning. I kept an eye open for the information Beverly insisted was true, but never found any reference to it.

I was not too interested in the content of Beverly's new information, about which I was very skeptical because it wasn't in any of the books I looked at. But it set me to pondering a different question: If I could prove a fact by pointing to it in a book, how could I *disprove* a *non-fact*? To this day, that question intrigues me every time it arises.

My First Bicycle

❦

The summer I was 12, in 1945, World War II ended and the ban on manu-facturing bicycles was lifted. From 1941, when America entered the war to save the world, all metal was used to build tanks and planes. That's why I never had a two-wheeler. My playmate Danny had a bike; if I pleaded hard enough, he would sometimes let me try to ride it.

There was a house between mine and his that had a large rock at the corner of the driveway. The first times I rode his bike, I told myself I would roll past the rock. But what I was really thinking was, "Don't hit that rock!" I'd stare at the rock and every time would steer right into it, ending up with a skinned knee. Danny would yell at me for scratching his bike. Then I would apologize and go home in tears to get a bandage for my bleeding knee.

Eventually I learned that the best way to not fall was to think about staying on the sidewalk rather than staring at the rock. We had to ride our bikes on the sidewalk if we were under 12; that was the law—at least, that was what my mother told me. In those days, kids' bikes didn't have speed gears or hand brakes. You just pedaled to go forward; to stop, you pedaled backward, which set the brake against the wheel. Because Danny's was a boy's bike, I had to learn how to jump off without hitting the crossbar when I stopped.

Once bicycles were being manufactured again, my parents agreed that it was time I had my own. I was very excited the day my father said we would go for a bike.

"How are you going to get the bike home?" my mother wanted to know.

"We'll figure it out. Don't worry about it," my father said. "Judy, get in the car."

So off we went to the bike store. It was straight up Woodrow Wilson, next to a gas station, maybe 10 blocks from our street. The man at the store found a girl's model that was the right size for me. I picked a bright blue one, my favorite color, always. The man blew up the tires, my father paid him and the bike was mine.

"Daddy, how *are* we going to get it home?" I asked. It was now obvious to me, as it had been earlier to my mother, that it would not fit into a car.

"You are going to ride it," my father said. "Just follow my car."

"You mean ride it *in the street?*" I asked, incredulous.

"Yes, just be careful."

So we rode in a procession of two, my father driving slowly and I pedaling directly behind his car. I was very excited to be allowed to ride in the street. There was almost no traffic, but I knew my mother would not allow it if she were there. We arrived home safe and victorious, and all the kids on the block were envious.

My mother was relieved to see us home safely, but then she started in: "Herman, how could you let her ride behind you? What if a car had bumped into her? You wouldn't have been able to do a thing about it!" She was quite angry. It almost spoiled my excitement, but she was angry at him, not me, so I concentrated on my bike.

"Judy, I will NOT allow you to ride in the street," she said emphatically. Stay on the sidewalk or I'll take the bike away."

Owning the bike gave me freedom I had never experienced. I was happy to stay on the sidewalk so long as I could leave the house. Although riding on the sidewalk, at any age, was actually against a city ordinance, my mother's law superseded the city's. I rode to visit friends a few blocks away, I rode purely for the pleasure of movement, feeling the breeze in my face and, best of all, I could ride to the public library.

Duffield Branch Library was on West Grand Boulevard at the foot of Twelfth Street. I rode from Virginia Park down Twelfth Street, about 12 blocks south, bumping up and down the curbs at every corner. In the 1940's, Detroit still was safe enough for children to play outdoors alone and to ride a bike without fear of being kidnapped or having the bike hijacked. At the library, for good measure, I parked my bike in a bike rack and locked it with a combination lock and chain.

I loved reading as much as bike riding. Once in the library, I looked up my favorite authors and checked out several books at a time. My bike had a basket on the handlebars large enough to hold them all. It had been exhilarating to be able to go somewhere without my mother and now I could spend the rest of the afternoon happily on the porch, reading.

Family

～

Parents
Grandparents
My Brother
Mother and I

Parents

∾

Evelyn Apple, my mother, was born in Detroit in 1907, the younger of two sisters, daughters of Fanny and Louis Apple. Her early photos show an exceptionally pretty girl with long wavy hair. She was a red-head, which in those days was a status that drew teasing rather than compliments; at least, she recalled being called "carrot-top" by other children. Her older sister, Elizabeth, was also pretty, with long dark hair.

Evelyn went to the "old" Central High School (which later became "Old Main" on the Wayne University campus). She was a good student, and had many talents and interests: she liked to act, dance, ice skate, paint, play the piano and sing. She was an avid reader. In high school she made friends whom she continued to see throughout her adult life.

When Elizabeth and then Evelyn finished high school, each went to work. Elizabeth went into retailing and became a buyer of women's clothes for The B. Siegel Company, a thriving department store in downtown Detroit. Evelyn thought that Elizabeth had a glamorous life because she traveled to New York repeatedly for her buying trips. Evelyn's clothes were chosen for her by her sister (at a discount) all of her life. She appreciated that, but as a result she developed no confidence in her own taste.

Evelyn learned shorthand and became a stenographer for the Detroit Public Library. It was a job she was proud of; whenever she took me, as a child, to the Main Branch, she pointed out where she had worked. Although she had been a top student in high school and wanted to go to college, she didn't have that opportunity. Her warm and jovial father had a major failing: while traveling 'on the road' to sell jewelry, he had too many opportunities to drink and gamble at cards. Evelyn's parents needed the money she brought home to pay the debts that Louis incurred.

Evelyn studied French during and beyond her teen years and longed to travel, especially to France, where she had corresponded as a child with her Uncle Max, Louis' brother. When she was in her teens, Max wrote to invite her to visit him and his family in their home near Paris. Her mother would not allow her to travel alone to the very continent from which she herself had escaped at the same age. For my mother, to visit France became a life-long, unfulfilled dream.

When Evelyn was in her early 20's, she was introduced to a well-known local journalist, Herman Wise.

Herman, like Evelyn, was the child of Jewish parents who had emigrated from Eastern Europe as teenagers and met in the United States. The oldest of six siblings, he was born in Montreal, Canada in 1903. When he was still a baby, his parents moved to Peekskill, NY, and later to Great Falls, Montana, before settling in Detroit.

Herman was a fastidious child who hated life outdoors in the country. An old family story was that even as a very young child, Herman wouldn't sit down on the porch stoop until he had cleaned it off, fearful of getting dirt on his short white pants. While his younger brothers, John and Leo, loved to ride horses, Herman preferred to stay indoors reading or practicing the violin. If he failed to practice for a full hour, his father spanked him, hard. As Herman entered his teens, he began to call his father "George" and took over disciplining his younger siblings as though he were the father. His younger sisters loved, respected and obeyed him. One winter everyone in the family except Herman became very ill with influenza, and Herman helped his weakened father take care of the entire family.

When Herman was old enough for high school, George moved his family back east to Detroit, where many of his relatives were now living. Herman went to Eastern High School. He was an excellent student and a good writer. When he graduated he went to the University of Michigan, where he studied journalism. He was still studying violin, as well.

After graduating from U. of M., Herman was hired as a reviewer by the Detroit Free Press, in those days a prestigious newspaper. Before long he became their music critic. He also, at various times, covered drama, travel and art and wrote book reviews. A handsome young man, he had his own daily column with his photograph and byline at the top. Being a reviewer for a major city newspaper was a highly respected job.

One of his more special assignments was to interview the Mexican artist Diego Rivera, who was painting a large mural, depicting the rise of industrialism, in the courtyard of the Detroit Institute of Arts. Because Rivera worked high on a scaffold, he told this young reporter to meet him at a particular date and time at his hotel. As the story was told years later, when my father arrived, Rivera was soaking in the bathtub. He insisted that my father conduct the interview then and there, while he was relaxing. It was unconventional, but my father complied.

Evelyn and Herman were introduced by mutual friends. She was four years his junior, and immediately smitten by this good looking, intelligent man, well known from his newspaper columns, who commanded much respect and who wrote about all the things she loved. He was equally attracted to Evelyn's beauty, intelligence, and the interest she showed in him. When she was 22 and he was 26, they married.

On their honeymoon, they drove to Montreal. My mother was very excited about being able to use her knowledge of French.

"We got lost and stopped to ask a policeman the way. I asked in my best French but the policeman just said, 'Talk English, Lady!' I was so disappointed!"

In 1933, four years after their marriage, I was born. Evelyn and Herman were thrilled to have a baby daughter, and felt fortunate that Herman had a good job to support the three of us at a time when so many people were out of work. Because Herman and Evelyn had watched their own parents lose their homes during the early Depression years, they were afraid to invest in buying a house, choosing to rent instead.

We had been living in the upstairs flat on Virginia Park for two years when my father was offered another job. The Detroit Symphony Orchestra was expanding, and needed someone to head up a new publicity department. My mother was reluctant to have him give up the prestige of his newspaper column, but he felt this was a new and exciting opportunity, wanted the higher salary, and made the move.

I liked his new position. He took me to all the children's concerts at Orchestra Hall and I felt "special" not sitting with the school groups, but being in a box seat with my father. I liked the name of his new job, even though it was a mouthful to say: "Publicity Director of the Detroit Symphony Orchestra." I was very proud to walk into his new office holding his hand.

Then, in 1941, the United States entered World War II, and there was no longer any funding for the Detroit Symphony. The Symphony disbanded and my father was out of a job. Ironically, because of a union he had helped start at the Free Press, he was unable to get his old job back.

My parents were in turmoil. My mother said, "I told you not to leave the paper!" My father suddenly had no patience with any of us, and read the newspapers a lot. My brother and I had to be very quiet. My mother was highly emotional and angry with my father. "He's always been so moody," she said to me often, in exasperation. "Don't ever marry a man who is moody!" I heard this line for many years.

Eventually my father was hired by the Automobile Manufacturers Association (AMA). He did public relations work for them and was the writer/editor of their newsletter. He made close friends in the office. At that time George Romney, who later became governor of Michigan, was president of the company. He was a kind man, good to work for. Life grew comfortable again for my parents throughout most of the 1940s, before the tides turned again.

Jenny and George Wise (paternal grandparents)

Fanny and Louis Apple (maternal grandparents)
with Judy, age 6

Grandparents

༃

One of my early blessings was four grandparents who loved me. As the first grandchild on both sides of my family, I was adored.

My parents used the tradition of calling grandparents by their last names: hence there were Grandma and Grandpa Apple (my mother's parents) and Grandma and Grandpa Wise (my father's). My grandfather's name was not really Wise, I was later told, it was Wasserman. When he stepped off the boat from Europe to enter the United States, the people at immigration couldn't spell the longer name, so they shortened it.

Both sets of grandparents lived within walking distance of our house when I was very young, so we visited back and forth frequently. My relationship with each of them varied in quality and depth. Each of them was born in Europe, in the changing territory that was either Russia or Romania, and experienced the poverty and fear of their Jewish ghetto life. They all left their own families as teenagers and suffered arduous journeys to seek freedom and prosperity in the United States. I regret the lost opportunity of asking them to tell me stories about their lives. It was something none of them spoke about. In my family, the phrase was, *"Shah, der kinder!"* ("Quiet, the children!")

Maybe, even if I had asked, they wouldn't have told me much.

Grandpa Apple

When Grandpa Apple (Louie, as my father called him) comes over on Sunday morning he brings love and smiles along with the bagels. My mother seems very happy when her father is in the house.

Grandpa lets me sit in his lap. I rest my back against his round belly and he puts an arm around me so I won't slide off. "Let Grandpa eat his breakfast," my mother says, but Grandpa says, "I can eat with one hand. Judy can stay right here."

When we finish eating, he takes me with him on a walk to Twelfth Street for a shoeshine. The shoeshine chairs are very high. We each sit in one and I watch as the man with dark brown skin shines Grandpa's shoes with black shoe polish. When he is done Grandpa gives the man some money and lifts me down from the chair. Then we stop at the newspaper stand to purchase the *Forverts*, the Yiddish newspaper. It has funny marks for words instead of letters I can read. We hold hands and talk as we walk down the street, I with my patent leather shoes and plump curls, he in his long overcoat. We make one more stop, at the store that has penny candy, and I choose my favorite, a Tootsie Roll. He is my favorite of all my grandparents.

It is the afternoon of Halloween, six months after my ninth birthday. I am thinking excitedly about this evening, when I will go out "begging" with my little brother and the other kids on the block. Daddy always walks along with us, waiting on the sidewalk as we run up to people's doors to get our candy.

The phone rings. Mother answers and bursts into tears. I watch, frightened.

"What's wrong? Who called?" I want to know.

"Grandpa Apple. He . . ." she whispers something to my father, who tells me gently, "Grandpa just had a heart attack on his front porch. He died right away."

Mother is weeping. Daddy tells me, "Walk Mommy to her room. She's very sad." My mother and I put our arms around each other's waists and walk down the hallway to her bedroom, where she enters alone. I hear her crying through the closed door.

Daddy is on the phone talking about a funeral. I don't know what to do or where to be. I feel confused and left out. He is my Grandpa, not only Mommy's father. I feel angry that there is no one talking to me about Grandpa. I am supposed to comfort Mommy but I don't know how to, since she has shut her door. I don't understand her crying because I have no tears. The sadness is all hers. I go into my bedroom but I don't want to be there. It is still a nice afternoon; I think I will go down the stairway to outdoors and see what the other kids are wearing for Halloween.

As I approach the front door Mother comes out of her room. "I don't think she should be outside playing," she says to my father, who has just hung up the phone.

"Why not?" I ask. "I want to see what time Grace and Danny are going out begging."

"Your grandfather just died!" mother says, her eyes flashing. "You aren't going to go out for Halloween tonight."

At this, I run into my bedroom and fling myself on the bed, weeping. Why is Mommy mad at me? Why can't I go out on Halloween like everyone else? It's not fair, any of it. Why did Grandpa have to pick today to die? What does dying mean, anyway? I sob into my pillow, trying not to be heard.

Daddy comes into my room and sits beside me on the bed. He rests his hand lightly on my shoulder. "Try not to cry now," he says. "Mommy is very sad and she needs you to help her."

"What happened to Grandpa?" I am finally able to ask.

Daddy explains: "Grandpa had a heart attack. He was on his front porch trying to open the door with his key. His heart stopped beating and he fell down. When Grandma opened the door later she found him there. He must have died right away.

"But why can't I go out begging tonight?" I ask. I don't see what one thing has to do with the other.

"When someone in the family dies, it is a sign of respect to not do certain things. I won't go to the office tomorrow, either."

"Do I get to stay home from school?" At last, a bright spot.

"We'll see, dear, we'll see. Now come out and be with your mother."

The day is ruined. The evening is boring. Mommy and Daddy are on the phone all the time, Mommy is crying a lot, Dick and I are sent to our rooms. I think about my friends who are out having fun. Our doorbell keeps ringing as other children come for candy. It all seems so unfair. *If Grandpa were here*, I think, *he would give me a big hug and take me out begging himself.* That is the moment when I realize the meaning of "Grandpa died." I put on my pajamas, get into bed and cry into my pillow.

The next morning, my parents dress in very dark clothes and leave the house to go to the funeral. They don't think it is "necessary" for children to go to a funeral, so I have to stay home with Dick and a neighbor lady they asked to stay with us. Dick is only five, but I think they could have taken me. This just proves what I thought in the first place, that all the sadness belongs to my mother and I'm not supposed to feel anything.

If this is true, then what my mother asks me to do later makes no sense to me at all. I have a box filled with shiny silver dollars that Grandpa has given me over the past few years. Sometimes I buy something with them and sometimes I save them. When my mother comes home from the funeral, she asks me where the last silver dollar is. "It's in the box with the others," I say, puzzled. "I'm saving up for something." I didn't know what that would be, but I could decide later.

"I want you to save those coins forever," Mother says. "They were your last presents from Grandpa. If you keep them, you'll always have something of him that he gave to you."

I'm not planning to spend them any time soon, but being told I can't only confirms what I believe to be true: my feelings don't count, Grandpa's death belongs to Mother, not to me, and even the money he gave me is not really mine. No one would understand how angry, sad and confused I feel but Grandpa.

And now I can never tell him.

Grandma Apple

Walking home from Hutchins Intermediate School, I pass the apartment building where my mother's mother (Fanny) lives, now that Grandpa is gone. Several times a week I stop in to visit. She is happy to see me and offers me cookies and milk. She asks me how school was, but doesn't really listen to the answer. She is more interested in telling me how her back is hurting. I know she loves me, but our conversations are either about food or about her problems.

Once I stop in with my girlfriend, who has an artist's eye even in 8th grade, and who comments on what was once the beauty of Grandma's face. I've never noticed; I've only seen a slightly hunched, gray haired woman with wrinkled skin and an unhappy attitude. With my friend's comment in front of me, I see that Grandma has a finely shaped nose, high cheekbones and a well- shaped mouth. Perhaps, 30 or 40 years ago, with long black hair, she was a beauty. It is hard for me to tell, now. To me, she simply looks old.

Grandma seems to me to complain a lot. Her back hurts, her head aches, and the famous line in our family is, "I didn't sleep a whole night!" If we were to believe this, Grandma hasn't slept at all in several years. Yet everyone in our house has witnessed her asleep on our sofa at times, snoring loudly. So her complaints are not taken seriously by the rest of the family.

Grandma Apple is a good cook. When she still lived in the downstairs flat of her two-family house, before she moved into this small apartment, we spent many Friday nights at her house for dinner. (That is, my mother, my brother and I ate there. Daddy never went with us. It was another thing I never questioned and that was not explained to me, since "children don't need to know.")

Walking with Dick and my mother to Grandma's house, I was thinking only of her chicken noodle soup, one of my favorite dishes in the world. When we arrived, the table was filled with bowls of food: boiled chicken, mashed potatoes, peas and carrots, fresh *challah* (egg bread) and home-made applesauce. Grandma always gave us the choice of eating the soup first, or later, after the chicken. I always asked for the soup first, please.

One of my favorite gifts was given to me by Grandma Apple: a black stuffed Scotch terrier. He had a button in his side that could be pushed to make him "bark." I named him Scottie, and he slept on my bed until I got married. By then, one ear was ripped and he could no longer make a sound. I could not leave him behind, however. With my husband's under-standing, he moved into our first apartment with us. He survived until my children were toddlers, when his stuffing began to come out, and we had to say goodbye. I always associated Scottie with Grandma's love for me. She knew how much I wanted a dog of my own.

As Grandma got older, her behavior changed. She accused my mother of things my mother did not do. "You stole my kitchen knives," she screamed one afternoon at our house. My mother screamed back, and then wept. I hid behind the swinging door that separated the dining room from the kitchen. I don't think my mother, in the 1940's, knew any more about dementia or paranoia than I did. She must have felt terribly abused and betrayed by the strange accusations and unaccountable rages of her own mother.

From stories I heard from my mother about her own childhood, Grandma was always feisty and often angry. At the age of fifteen, she had left her own family in the Russian ghetto and snuck off to board a ship headed for the United States. Then she spent the rest of her life feeling guilty. When my mother told me this story, I had no way to understand it. I couldn't even think of questions to ask. (*What was the ship like? Did she get seasick? What did she do about money? What did she take with her? How did she know where to go when she got to New York? How did she make herself understood if she couldn't speak English? How did she and Grandpa meet?*) As an overprotected little girl who was scarcely allowed to go around the block by myself, the entire adventure was beyond the scope of my young imagination.

One day Grandma Apple fell and broke her hip. From the hospital she went into the "Jewish Old Folks Home," as the nursing home was generally referred to. She was still in her 60's, but seemed to me, in my early teens, like a very old woman. When she was in the nursing home, she had little to say to me; she spent her time complaining to my mother. Her hip never healed, and Grandma Apple died shortly after the accident.

Grandpa Wise

Grandpa Wise (George), my father's father, sits in his wheel chair, gesturing to me to come closer and give him a kiss. I am six years old, and I approach him with shyness and discomfort. He gestures to me with one hand, but cannot move the other. He smiles from one side of his face but the other side does not move. One eye follows me but the other stares straight ahead. I don't know whether to kiss him on the side that moves or the other side. He speaks to me but I don't understand his words. I sense that he loves me, yet I feel frightened about touching him.

I'm sad that I remember only this. Grandpa's stroke happened the year I was born. My father, writing about it, said that George's only joy after that time was in his grandchildren (by the time I was six, there were three others: Carolyn (Jack's daughter), Dick (my brother) and Bob (Leo's son). I'm sure he would not have wanted me to feel fear or discomfort around him. Probably this memory is vivid because the scene was repeated each time I saw him.

Some time before my seventh birthday, Grandpa Wise dies. I am not included in the funeral or *shiva*, if there was one. The next time I visit at Grandma's apartment, there is no wheelchair. No Grandpa who wants me to give him a kiss. More than loss, I feel relief.

My father, Herman, wrote an unpublished piece about his father, George. It is included next, unedited, as he wrote it in 1938. George died a year later.

My Father
By Herman Wise

When, in 1913, the United States Government offered citizens large tracts of free acreage in the west for farming purposes, my father, always eager to explore new business pastures, decided he would investigate.

In the village where we then lived, an hour by rail from New York City, my father operated a small soda water plant, manufacturing what is now commonly known as pop. He did all the work himself—bought the materials, took charge of the mixing, handled the bottling and ran the deliveries.

As I recall it, the Peekskill Bottling Works was rather a good business and eventually (as actually happened to his only competitor) might have enabled my father to gather a tidy sum for his old age.

But my father has never been blessed with old-time patience. He has always wanted things to happen in a hurry. That is why he was always seeking something new in a business way. The soda water business was venture number six in a list of endeavors that could easily total fifteen at which, at one time or another, my father tried his hand and brain.

Against the wishes of my mother, a more conservative and wiser soul, the determined head of the family mortgaged his business and prepared to "go west." He would look over the situation for a brief period and send for my mother and the four children later.

In due time, my mother and the four of us, the oldest 10, started for Montana, traveling some 2500 miles by day coach and carrying our food supply in a large covered clothes basket which also contained the clean diaper supply for the youngest of the children, a babe in arms.

We arrived in Great Falls only to learn that my father had decided not to accept the government's generous offer and that for the time being, at least, we would settle in the city.

81

My father explained that his investigation of dry land farming in Montana had convinced him that while such an activity might be well for those who were interested, it certainly would not be to his liking. He had been told too much about the nearly ever-present drouth, too much about the endless laboring for which there was little or nothing to show at the end of the year. This, plus the fact that my father had never been a farmer and that his lack of patience would not permit him to wait around for doubtful crops, caused him to make what proved to be a wise decision.

After a time as an upholsterer, during which he built himself a huge workshop made almost entirely of boards from packing boxes, my father started in the fruit business. The workshop, with the rear of our four room cottage serving as the north wall, was converted into a storage place. My father would buy large quantities of fruit that had ripened too fast in the commission houses and have it sold from house to house by hired men. This business had action and pleased him. But after three or four years, when local shipments became smaller and competition increased, my father decided to try something else. This time it was the retail grocery and meat business.

For a few months all went well, but the beginning of a four-year drouth had set in and soon began to have its effects on my father's business as well as on all others. Surrounded as it was by dry land farmers upon whom local merchants depended for a good share of their business, Great Falls began to experience a depression of its own.

The great epidemic of influenza came in the midst of the drouth years. It took a heavy toll of life in Great Falls and naturally helped crush business. By now, 1918, my father operated a garage. To be sure, he knew nothing about the business; he knew even less about the mechanics of an automobile. The grocery and meat business, like many others, had become history, and my father, with his characteristic courage and zeal, had to find a way to support his wife and children, the latter now numbering six. The garage business, of course, held no greater mystery than any other for the head of the family.

It was the influenza epidemic that helped force my father out of the garage business. Not only were he and my mother very ill, so were five of the six children. I remember how my father, himself stricken, labored over one brother and sister who were nearer death's door than the rest. Nothing daunted my father, not even the great epidemic. I am satisfied that in his own unprofessional and crude manner, my father did as much to save the lives of my brother and sister as any doctor could have under the circumstances.

Each succeeding year of the drouth had made it more difficult to make a living in Montana. Farmers were deserting their homesteads, leaving behind half-starved livestock and sad-appearing shanties. The population of Great Falls began to decrease sharply.

Opportunity for one such as my father, a man who had never taken an order from a superior, practically ceased.

The idea of moving again began to take root. It required only slight urging on the part of relatives in Michigan to help my father make up his mind. With a few hundred dollars in his pockets, about the same amount with which a few years before he had set out for the west and possible fortune, my father, together with my mother and the six children, headed for Detroit. The day coach once more was the means of travel. This time, however, there was no clothes basket in which to carry food. We were equipped with more or less dignified appearing suitcases.

In Detroit it was the furniture business which attracted attention and for a number of years my father managed to eke out a living, working long and hard for what he earned. Then followed several years in which my father's ability as an auctioneer brought in the means necessary to pay for food, clothing and rent. This work, too, became dull for my father.

Even the beginning of the Depression found my father considering new business moves. However, there were to be no new ventures because, for once, my father found himself face to face with an all-too-powerful enemy, ill health. Inactivity and financial worry, coupled with a deeply-felt disappointment at not being able for the first time in his life to cope with a business problem, completely defeated my father. This defeat was to prove itself everlasting, for in 1933, after two long years of not being able to adjust himself, my father suffered a cerebral stroke, resulting in a paralysis of his entire right side.

This, of course, was a wholesale crush, and were he able to at the time, my father would have done away with himself. After six months of living death my father was permitted to get out of bed and with this improvement came a slightly different attitude toward things. For several years now, much to the surprise of the doctors who in the beginning felt my father would never leave his bed, this former American business man has managed to get about by himself, although he remains extremely weak physically and cannot engage in work of any kind.

For one who has been active in business all his life, and my father insists that he first started in business for himself when he ran away from home at the age of seven, the present existence is a little more than hopeless. The keenest interest my father has, perhaps the one that permits him to tolerate his condition at all, is his four grandchildren. The comfort he derives from a visit with them appears sufficient for him to carry on for days or even weeks, albeit he realizes each visit with them may be his last.

Only in the United States, certainly, could my father have had his experiences. With its widespread borders, its peoples of all lands and its opportunities as numerous as its ambitions, this fascinating country enabled my father to carry on his rather aimless life with few tears or heartaches. That he was stricken is no fault of the land to which he emigrated before the opening of the century. It would have happened anywhere, for this was the established price my father could not escape paying nature for his impatience and over-indulgence.

Grandma Wise

My father's mother, Grandma Wise (Jenny), was a short woman with a round face, short, wavy gray hair and glasses. Her voice was soft and her manner gentle. She never seemed to yell or get upset. She was the one who baby-sat for me and my brother when my parents went out at night. A sweet, somewhat passive woman, she allowed me to take advantage of her kindness. With Grandma Wise in charge and my parents away, I jumped on the furniture, leapt from one chair to another, walked across the rounded back of the green sofa in the living room, ran up and down the bedroom hallway and sang at the top of my lungs. These were sins of exuberance for which I would have been seriously punished if my parents knew, and which I never would have dared to do in their presence. Invariably, my little brother joined me in this forbidden behavior. Grandma tried, sweetly and ineffectually, to get us to stop.

She never told on us. Did I thank her? No, I insisted she play cards with me. It was Grandma Wise who taught me to play Casino. The moment she walked into our house I had the deck of cards out, ready to keep her my captive. She was always accommodating. I felt safe with her and knew she loved me even when I misbehaved.

I suppose, in the overall picture of her difficult life, my behavior was the least of her troubles. She never complained or talked about her past, and it never occurred to me to ask her any of the hundreds of questions that I thought of as an adult, when it was years too late to ask anyone. Jenny Sweet came to America from Russia when she was a teenager. She married George Wise, an energetic man with more ideas than perseverance, a man who was always on the move, changing cities and businesses at the slightest whim.

Jenny had two miscarriages before her second son, my Uncle Jack, was born, four years after Herman. My guess is that her grief and physical exhaustion must have turned into depression. Two years after Jack she had Leo, and then Rose. When Rose was still an infant, they all moved to Montana. While in Montana, Jenny bore two more children, Leone and Mary.

Rose, meanwhile, was not developing normally. In those days, it was considered shameful to have a retarded child, and there was no one to whom Jenny could turn for help. Also during those difficult years, my grandfather's livelihood suffered. After five years in Montana, George decided to move to Detroit, where he had many relatives. So Jenny packed up everything they could carry, and traveled once again by train across the country, this time with her husband and six children. Rose was becoming more unmanageable. After a few years in Detroit, unable to cope with this nearly adolescent daughter, they moved her to a State home.

Jenny's trials did not end with giving up her daughter. In 1933, the year I was born, when George suffered a stroke that left him paralyzed on one side, as well as depressed with suicidal wishes, Jenny was his full-time caregiver during the next six years of his life.

After George died was the time I remember Grandma Wise most clearly. She lived around the block from us in a small apartment that she shared with Mary, her youngest child. Most of my memories with her, such as when she baby-sat for us, are in the years when I was between six and perhaps 13. By the time I was in my teens and didn't need a baby sitter, Grandma had begun to deteriorate physically and mentally. She suffered from dementia and incontinence. For several years she went to live with Uncle Jack and Aunt Sunny, who cared for her until her symptoms were too severe even for their loving attention. Jenny sometimes left their house and was found wandering the streets around Livernois and Seven Mile Road, "going to visit her sister" (who had remained in Russia and was now dead).

Fearful for her safety, Jack and Sunny moved Jenny into the same care facility where Grandma Apple lived. My family visited every Sunday afternoon. My two grandmas sat in a hallway filled with wheelchairs, lined up with a dozen other old ladies. The hallway smelled of urine. Sometimes Grandma Wise recognized us but often we could not tell if she even knew we were there. She spoke very little, even to answer my parents' questions. She no longer was the same grandma who had played cards with me. She seemed like a very old lady now: bent over, white haired, unresponsive, drooling slightly. I dutifully said "Hello" when we arrived and kissed her goodbye when we were leaving. In between I was bored and miserable. I hated the Sunday visits and could not wait until we left the stuffy building to be outside in the fresh, clean smelling air. Just as I had with Grandpa Wise, I felt more relief than grief when she finally died. I took care of my guilt by imagining that perhaps she did, too.

My Brother

~

Dick and Judy, ages 2 and 6

When my mother went to the hospital to have my baby brother, she stayed there for ten days. During that time, my father's sister, Aunt Leone, took care of me. She was still single and lived around the block from us with her parents. My outstanding memory of this time was the day she washed my hair. In the rinsing process, shampoo got into my eyes. I screamed and cried for my mother. Aunt Leone kept explaining that Mommy was at the hospital and couldn't come to me, so then I cried for Daddy. He, of course, was at the office writing newspaper stories, but at least he talked to me on the telephone and told me he would be home at dinner time. That was not much comfort to a four-year-old in pain.

I longed for my mother to come home soon. When she finally did, there was a strange woman in the house, a nurse in a white uniform. She was there to help Mommy and to show her how to take care of the baby. To me, her main task seemed to be to keep me out of my mother's bedroom so she could rest. I snuck in anyway.

It was a long time between when my mother first left for the hospital to have the baby, and the day when I could finally see and touch my little brother. After all the deprivation, this occasion did not seem like a wonderful reward.

As Dick grew older, and could sit up by himself, I was more interested in him. From photos, I see that he was a beautiful little boy with dark, curly hair. Most of the time that he was awake, he was put into a playpen, which had a wooden floor with high rails. There were toys in the playpen, and I remember wanting to play with him and with the toys, so I climbed in. I had only good feelings toward my brother at that moment, but our mother, trying to fix dinner in the kitchen, must have been very nervous that I would somehow hurt him, and made me climb back out.

There is a photo of us together at ages two and six. I am wearing my best party dress and have long curls. Dick is wearing some sort of romper suit. We are in the backyard, and I recall my mother trying to get him to sit on a little chair long enough for her to take the picture. I am beside him, on bent knee, trying to encourage him to sit still for a minute, while my mother is scolding me for interfering with him. I recall feeling very loving toward my brother at that moment and confused by my mother's irritation. Eventually the photo was taken successfully.

During our elementary school years, my brother and I often fought. Sometimes it was verbal but often it was physical. I felt at a disadvantage: I was older and stronger, and perhaps could have stopped my brother's attacks, but I was afraid to hurt him. How would I ever explain it if I broke his skinny arm? I don't know what created so much rage in my brother toward me, but I can guess:

I was the favored child. I was a girl, and quieter. Neither of my parents had any tolerance for disruption or chaos in their lives, and two children create infinitely more than one. When I played with my girlfriends, many of whom had younger brothers, we closed Dick out of my bedroom. He must have felt terribly hurt to be excluded. To us, it seemed standard fare: we closed out all the younger brothers. But Dick had no way of knowing that, or caring, when he was the target of rejection.

As the oldest child, I went many places with my parents that Dick was too young for: concerts, children's theater productions, ice skating with my mother or on long walks from our house to the Fisher Building for lunch and shopping. Even though Dick was too young to join us, he may have felt left out, as indeed he was.

Worst of all was my parents' habit of making comparisons. I am sure they held me up as an example ("Why are you making such a mess? Judy is so neat when she plays.") I recall that my mother's friend's daughter, Lois Luskin, was constantly held up to me: "Lois baked cookies today and cleaned up the entire kitchen herself." I did not know how to bake and my mother would never trust me alone in her kitchen. I hated Lois Luskin for being so perfect. I imagine my brother felt the same way about me.

Our father was a perfectionist, obsessive about neatness and order, and could be quite impatient, especially during the low swings of his emotional cycle. I came in for my share of criticism for incorrect grammar, misspelled words and out-of-tune violin playing. I believe that Dick was much more severely reprimanded, and more often, than I.

One day all four of us went with another family, whose children's ages matched ours, on an outing to Belle Isle. It was spring, and the ground was still muddy. Dick was about three. We took a picnic lunch and found a table near a playground which had swings and a merry-go-round. I was having a wonderful time eating peanut butter and jelly sandwiches and playing tag with my girlfriend, when I heard loud crying. Dick had decided to get off the merry-go-round while it was still in motion, and had fallen on his face in a big mud puddle. He was covered from head to toe with mud. Mother said later that she couldn't even find a clean spot to kiss him. My parents quickly wiped him off, threw all the picnic stuff in the car, and we left for home to give him a bath. I, with notable lack of compassion, was furious that he had spoiled our fun.

Dick's best friend from age four until his teen years was Geoff, the younger brother of my friend Suzy, who lived just across the street. The two boys spent hours playing with toy cars and trucks on the dining room floor of Geoff's house. Geoff's father was a trucker, and Geoff knew a lot of trucking lingo. They called each other by names such as "Joe" and "Mike" as they conducted their long-distance hauling. I suspect that these were among the happiest hours of Dick's childhood.

Once, when my brother was 10 and I was 14, he came to me sweetly with a question. Our parents were out for a brief evening walk and I was in my bedroom. In an unusual gesture of good will, he knocked politely on my door, which was partly open. I don't recall the exact content of our discussion, but it had to do with clarifying confusing sexual information he had received from some older kids. I was pleased that he trusted me enough to ask and I tried to be very respectful and gentle in answering him. It surprised me a little that he had not asked our parents, but I intuitively understood why. I had hopes that this would be the start of peace in our relationship, but we soon fell back into our normal squabbling.

When Dick was about nine or ten, he saved enough money from his allowance and from working around the house to pay for a football that he had coveted. It was his pride and joy. Eventually, as happens to footballs, it began to deflate. Dick had spent a lot of time at the corner gas station, and was friendly with one of the young men who worked there. When the football needed air, the man offered to put some in for him. He put in too much and the football exploded. I don't remember his reaction or how my parents handled the situation, but I guess, from the pain I feel writing these words almost six decades later, that it was akin to a death.

As I became more immersed in high school and dating boys, I paid less and less attention to Dick, who was still in his last year of elementary school. The fateful year we moved from Virginia Park, when my father bought a new house, lost his job and fell into a depression, Dick was just ready to start Intermediate School in the new neighborhood. He had now lost daily contact with his best friend, Geoff, although he spent time with Geoff and his family in the summers. While there were many boys on our new block, they were all a year older and a lot bigger than he was. To my brother's credit, he did not give up, and within a year, having gained adolescent growth and a deeper voice, was "one of the gang." He had also developed a sense of clowning. Since he looked a bit like Jerry Lewis, the young and handsome entertainer, he gained popularity in school. With his new deep voice, he sang in the school glee club. Academics, however, were not his greatest interest, another area where he was undoubtedly compared to me by our parents.

While I handled the tense situation in our household the year we moved by immersing myself in college work and new friends, Dick, still in high school, probably had a more difficult time. By then our lives were very separate, although we lived under the same roof. Several years later, after I married and moved out of the house on Appoline, Dick was still living with our parents, who were dealing with financial difficulties and illnesses. By then his negativity and anger toward me were intense, although as I consider it now from another perspective, I may have been only a safe and convenient scapegoat for the years of feelings he was not allowed to express.

While in high school, Dick developed support networks with two other families: our aunt and uncle, my father's brother Jack and his wife, Aunt Sunny, and a young couple who lived across the street, Sybil and Dick Alvin. Each family had two young daughters, and I imagine that they enjoyed the company of this handsome, personable, teenage surrogate son. Both men were mentors to Dick, and the family relationships provided a degree of unconditional acceptance and reinforcement that was difficult to find at home. I believe our parents loved him very much, but were too entangled in their own problems to know how to communicate that to him.

After our mother died, Dick continued for a while to live in the same house with my father. We never spoke, then or later, about how that time was for him; what it meant to lose his mother when he was only 22; how both of us had felt growing up with our parents. Was the mother I knew the same one he knew? We have never had these sibling conversations.

Shortly after our mother died, Dick asked my husband for financial help. Bob was working for a law firm downtown and his office must have looked rather elegant. The reality was that Bob received a very low salary; we had a new house and baby and no savings. Bob and I talked over the request and felt unable to help him. What we didn't know for many years was how humiliated and abandoned by us Dick had felt at 22.

Shortly after that incident, a family friend offered Dick a job in his food brokerage company. Food brokers, in those days, were the "middle men" between manufacturers of food items and household products and the growing super market industry that sold those products. Dick worked his way up, over the years, to become a partner.

In the following years, we became increasingly estranged. When Dick married Diana and they adopted Geoffrey and Susan, I had hopes that we might become closer, but it didn't happen. Dick increasingly withdrew from us. He had very little contact with our children until they were well into adulthood. They, and later our grandchildren, scarcely knew they had an Uncle Dick. I was disappointed by the loss of relationship with my brother.

During the decade of the 1990's, long after both our parents had died, Dick, Diana and I cooperated in taking care of our father's second wife, Sharon. Gradually, as the frequency and quality of our contacts increased, Dick became more open to inclusion in family functions.

Happily, now that we are in our '70s, there is at last a warm relationship. Dick is happy to be with our extended family and we are happy to have him. My adult children are glad to finally get to know their Uncle Dick, and my grandchildren accept his presence with natural ease. When I became very ill in the early months of 2009, Dick was there almost every day to help us out: to drive me to doctor appointments, shovel snow for us, assist me going up a stairway or getting out of the car on icy pavement. I felt his genuine warmth and caring.

I think both of us matured as we recognized the shortness of life and the good fortune of having a sibling. We are now the "older generation" in the family. I know that I am happy to have my brother back in my life.

Mother and I

❦

As a brand new mother, Evelyn tried to follow all the rules. She was quite anxious. She told me this when I had my first baby, Gary. When she brought me home from the hospital she was afraid to give me a bath, lest I slip from her arms, and hired a nurse to teach her how to do it safely. In 1933, the current advice was to feed the baby every four hours, even if she cried sooner. Uncomfortable with nursing, she chose to bottle-feed me, and obediently adhered to the schedule.

When I was a toddler and young child, life was good between my mother and me, although even then there were negative moments. One of my earliest memories takes place at a lake where my parents have taken me for a family vacation. It's the summer following my third birthday. I'm with my parents, but suddenly my mother isn't there. Upset, I ask Daddy where she went, but he is vague and only says, "She's coming right back." I feel anxious and worried; I cry and keep asking him where she is, but receive no real answer. Soon she emerges, dripping wet: she had gone for a swim in the lake. As an adult, I understand her need to swim without a three year old hanging on her. At that time, I only understood that she and my father had kept something from me. Why couldn't they have just said, "Mommy is swimming"? Of all my experiences at the lake that summer, this is the only one that stayed with me.

When I was in elementary school, we often took long walks together. At least, they seemed long to me. When my brother was a baby, napping, we left him with Leona, the teenage girl who lived with us as a mother's helper, and walked to the Euclid-Hamilton Market for groceries. Since my mother didn't drive, she only bought what we could carry home easily. Together we chose fresh fruit and a few staples and perhaps meat for dinner. It was a nice time to talk and simply be together.

In later childhood, when I could walk longer distances, we walked from our house on Virginia Park, just east of Twelfth Street, to the Fisher Building, a little over a mile. My mother pointed out the lovely architecture of the building. My pediatrician, Joe Himelhoch, had his office in that building for a while. Also, there was a children's shoe store where we went every spring to shop for new saddle shoes and black patent leather party shoes. Once we went to the "Golden Tower" on the top floor to see inside the radio broadcasting station, WJR. Sometimes we walked another long block to Woodward Avenue to shop at Demery's Department Store, or to have a hot fudge sundae at Sander's. It was an elegant place, Sander's, with a long ice cream bar and raised bar stools perched on a platform. When it was crowded, people lined up behind those already seated, peering over shoulders (or, for shorter children, between customers) to see who had the least amount of their sundae left, so as to get into the fastest line. It was always a huge decision whether to have vanilla ice cream or chocolate, and whether to order bittersweet topping or just plain hot fudge. Those are still among my favorite decisions in life.

At other times, Mother and I took the Woodrow Wilson bus to the Main Library or the Detroit Institute of Arts, or perhaps all the way downtown to shop at Hudson's Department Store and have lunch in the elegant dining room on the 13th floor. These were occasions to get "dressed up" rather than being in ordinary school clothes or play clothes. "Dressed up" meant black patent leather Mary Jane shoes, a skirt or dress, and sometimes a purse and little white gloves. These short cotton gloves had a button at the wrist and were worn spring and fall.

Often on Saturdays we teamed up with Mother's friend Molly, whose daughter, Elissa, was almost my age, and went to a children's concert or theater production. Molly had her own car and willingly picked us up for these events. Occasionally in the winter months another more athletic friend picked us up and we went ice skating with her children on the Detroit River at Belle Isle, or at Art Staff's local indoor rink. My mother was a graceful skater; I was usually skating on my ankles and fell down a lot, but she was patient about teaching me.

These outings were among my happy memories of times with my mother. She pointed out everything to me: art, architecture, books, music, theater, local history and current events that were in the newspaper or on the radio, as well as telling me stories of her own childhood. She tried hard to be the best wife and mother she could be. Her house and children were always immaculate and her meals as colorful and well-balanced as a culinary page from *The Ladies Home Journal*. She used every opportunity to instruct me in good manners, politeness, consideration for others, and morality tales. I received her pronouncements as law, and they remain with me to this day: "Don't tell the neighbors things that are going on in our house; it's none of their business." "Always send a nice thank-you note when someone gives you a gift." "Don't gossip."

As I moved into adolescence, our relationship was more problematic. Some of it had to do with events between my parents, of which I was only vaguely aware. Some of it was my mother's discomfort with my no longer being a little girl. There was much less hugging or kissing between us after I was 12. Intermediate School was not a very happy time for me. I was a year younger than my classmates and less physically developed, which made me the brunt of what is now referred to as 'bullying' by mean girls. There was no label for it then; I just endured. My unhappiness may have been expressed in my behavior and attitude at home and perhaps taken out on my mother.

What I recall with more clarity was high school, and my mother's on-going vigilance regarding boys and dating. I had an entire life that I didn't want to tell her about. She felt it was her job to protect and guide me. On more than one occasion she told me, with exasperation, "You know, everything you do reflects on me!" She was talking about her fear of what the neighbors would think if, for example, I sat too long in a date's parked car instead of coming directly into the house. To my credit, I somehow *knew* that we were not that entwined; that my behavior reflected only on me, not on her. But her belief was still like an invisible tether around my leg.

As an adult I understand her concerns, but in my teens we had constant skirmishes. My mother no longer had the company of the good little girl in patent leather shoes who held her hand walking to the Fisher Building. Instead, she had a moody, secretive adolescent daughter who might embarrass her in front of her friends and neighbors at any moment. Plus, her relationship with my father had tensions of its own which I felt but did not understand. Whenever I could, I spent time out of the house with my friends.

My high school years must have been very difficult for my mother. Her own mother was not well, her husband was becoming increasingly withdrawn, and her relationship with me was a source of constant friction. When I met Bob, during my first year in college, she relaxed a bit because she liked him, but by then the unspoken tensions between us were omnipresent. Her inability to say "I'm sorry" meant that, for me, unresolved issues carried over into the next day. She cheerfully said "Good morning" and I immediately felt angry. Her critical remarks to me felt more frequent and hurtful.

It was not until I wrote this that I remembered how different our earlier relationship had been and how loving a mother she was when I was little.

My mother's life did not end happily. When she was only 48, she found out that she had ovarian cancer. It was 1955, and treatment options were more primitive than today. By the time she was diagnosed, the cancer had metastasized. We were told she had "only a short time" left to live. However, my mother had a strong will. She wanted me to go to France with Bob, now my husband, in 1956 when his army unit was sent there, to live out her unfulfilled dream of meeting her French relatives. She didn't tell me how ill she really was, and I went. Next, she wanted to see me come home, although she later told me she didn't believe she would live that long. When I came home pregnant, she willed herself to live to see her first grandchild. She actually survived until age 52, four years beyond her initial diagnosis and a few months beyond Gary's first birthday.

My mother wanted to talk about her dying process, and I was unable to do that. In our household there had always been secrecy, denial, and pretending that things weren't really so bad, and that was all I knew at the time. My father never discussed anything painful in a direct way and my mother must have felt isolated in her attempts to communicate with us. A month before she died I bought her a gift of summer jewelry, even though we all knew she wouldn't live to see summer. I have always regretted that I didn't know how to speak directly and honestly to my mother in her last months.

It took me many years in therapy to work through the emotional pain of my relationship with my mother, as well as the pain I felt as I recognized how she had suffered and how I had contributed to her emotional isolation. Over the years after she died, I had many dreams about her. At first they

96

were dreams in which we were fighting, angry. Sometimes I woke up crying or shouting out loud. Eventually that changed, and the dreams became loving. I feel that somehow our relationship healed many years after her death, when I was well into adulthood. In some way which may be irrational and which I can't explain, I feel that the work of healing was mutual, and that she participated in it as much as I did.

Adolescence

ꙮ

Being Jewish: Intermediate School

⚬

Going to school on Jewish holidays was uncomfortable for me, especially during grades 7-9, my intermediate school years. All the Jewish kids stayed home, ostensibly to go to religious services. What they actually did, however, was get dressed up in their new fall suits and congregate outside the many Conservative and Orthodox synagogues that were in the neighborhood. While their parents were inside at services, my classmates were outside walking around, socializing and showing off their new clothes.

I could not join my school friends. Their families and synagogues were not part of the social framework of my parents' lives. Their religious lives were as different from mine as my life was from the religious world of my Christian friends. Furthermore, Rabbi Fram had declared from his pulpit at Temple Israel, if we stayed home from school, it should be only to attend religious services. Otherwise, we should be in school. I think he really meant that we should go to the services, but my parents heard this as an honest choice. By now, my Aunt Elizabeth no longer was a member of Temple Israel, so my choices were non-existent.

That's how I became the only Jewish kid in Hutchins Intermediate School on Rosh Hashanah in 1944 and had to answer questions about why all the other kids got to stay home, the lucky dogs. The worst part was the next day, when the Jewish kids came back. They treated me like a traitor: *You made us look bad; you aren't really Jewish; you should have stayed home like we did; who the heck is Rabbi Fram? What does he know?*

The next year my parents compromised: they let me stay home on the High Holidays (*Rosh Hashanah* and *Yom Kippur*) without attending services, but I had to go to school on the lesser holidays (*Simchat Torah, Sukkot* and *Shavuot*). I went through the same inquisition by the other kids on every holiday. It was not fun.

Frankfort: Age Thirteen

∽

We are, once again, in Frankfort, Michigan. I'm on my stomach on my beach towel, pretending I am asleep. My eyes are open when I think no one will notice. What I'm watching is a group of teenagers about five body-lengths away. They are all 15 and 16. The girls have on 2-piece bathing suits and the little halter tops show off their rounding breasts. The boys have fine hairs beginning to sprout on their chests and under their armpits. They are talking together, and laughing. I feel as if they are laughing at me, although I know they don't even know I'm there. I have just turned 13 and have almost no breasts beneath my halter top. I have to wear eyeglasses. My mother won't let me wear lipstick. I hide my face now, wishing I really were asleep, hoping no one will know I'm crying.

When the tears stop, I peek out again. A 15 year old boy named Tommy is running his index finger over the hill on the left side of Jennifer Rosen's chest. I can't stop staring, although I keep my head low on my folded arms. I know their names because their parents are friends of the family we are staying with. All the parents know each other, except mine. They all have enough money to rent their own houses for the summer and not have to be guests in someone else's house. I can't believe Jennifer is letting Tommy do this in broad daylight. She's laughing, too.

"Why don't you play with all these kids," my mother asked me yesterday. "They look nice." I just looked at her. Didn't she know they wouldn't even talk to a kid who was still in Intermediate School, only going into 9th grade? Watching them, now, I want to be Jennifer. I hate Jennifer.

Now they're all talking, loudly, about the party they had the night before, on the beach. A wiener roast, with marshmallows and beer.

"God, I got so drunk!" Jennifer is laughing.

"Yeah," says Joey Blumenthal, "you got so drunk you couldn't walk."

"Walk!" says Tommy, "All she could do was puke." Jennifer is lying on her back, giggling. Her feet are flat, knees pointed up, and I can see pubic hairs curling out from the crotch of her swimsuit.

My mother always told me a lady keeps her knees together. My mother also thought Jennifer was a Nice Girl and I shouldn't be so shy. My mother doesn't know anything.

I turn over and sit up, opening my book and facing away from them and toward the water. I'm reading *Anna Karenina*. Those dummies probably never even heard of it, I think to myself. Anna is with her lover now. I wonder if Jennifer lets Tommy touch the part where the pubic hairs show.

Low whitecaps are rolling onto the Lake Michigan beach, and the younger kids, my little brother and his friends, are jumping in and out of them. I used to do that, too, but in my two piece suit with no breasts and my new eyeglasses which the doctor said I would probably need forever, I cannot walk in full view of those teenagers.

When I think about walking, I remember what happened the month before we came on this vacation: I was walking near my house, feeling stiff and self conscious at the sound of voices behind me. I wanted to walk just like Diane, the most popular girl in homeroom. She was short and stocky with curly blonde hair. She talked and laughed a lot. I even tried to make my handwriting look like hers, a rounded back-slant that made my writing strange looking, as if someone else were inside of me doing the strokes. I thought if I could write and walk like Diane, maybe I could find the secret of why she was so popular. But I couldn't walk like Diane and I couldn't even walk like myself. And then this boy's voice behind me said to his companions, "Look at her, she looks like she's walking on stilts." My entire body stiffened and my face grew hot. I slowed down and let them pass me: two boys and a girl, probably in high school.

Now, I won't risk walking all the way to the shore even though I'm probably invisible to those kids. Instead, I sit facing the lake, watching the younger kids splash in the water, hearing the laughter of the group behind me, pretending that I'm crying about Anna. Thirteen, I know, is the most terrible age anyone could be. And I have no idea whether it will ever get any better.

Frankfort: Age Fifteen

෨

We are invited back to Frankfort again. I don't want to go.

"Those snotty kids will be there," I tell my mother. "There's nobody my age."

But mother entices me with surprise news. "Carl's cousin, Arnie, will be there." Arnie is almost 19, and goes to the University of Michigan. He is a musician. "He won a contest and he's playing the solo at Interlochen," she tells me. She remembers how unhappy I was on the last trip, and is playing her trump card. "Beethoven's 5th Piano Concerto. The Emperor Concerto. Arnie is the soloist. And we're all invited, on our way up."

I go to Cass Tech, a high school with separate departments for kids talented in music and art. I am not one of them, but they're my friends. She knows my intellectual snobbery cannot resist the concert invitation. "What does he look like," I want to know. "He's short, but he's nice look-ing," she reassures me. I'm not sure about Frankfort, but I'm excited about meeting a Real Musician who goes to the University of Michigan.

At 15, I've just completed 10th grade and a year of going around with a boy named Jimmy, who loved me a lot more than I cared for him. His mother was dead, and he reminded me of this at strategic moments. Our breakup was long and dragged out: I kept saying "This is our last date," and then he would cry and I would cry and hold him, and it would not be our last date. We repeated this scenario about three times between May and the end of June, when I finally found the strength to mean it. He was enraged and told all our friends stories about me, most of which were not true. I felt wounded, vulnerable and free.

We finally arrive at Interlochen Music Camp after the long, hot six hour ride in the Chevrolet. On the way up my mother had mentioned, very casually, that she wasn't sure, after all, if Arnie would be spending any time in Frankfort after the concert; she had thought he would, but found out that was not definite. I was terribly disappointed and felt betrayed, but determined not to let her know, convinced that anything she might say would only make me feel worse. Instead, I fantasized all the way up that when he met me, he would want to be in Frankfort. I had more confidence after a year with Jimmy.

Interlochen was in the woods and smelled of pine trees and damp earth. Kids and parents and tourists were all milling about the grounds before the concert, and there was a sense of electric excitement in the air. The concert was outdoors, and the soft breeze felt refreshingly cool. We were seated on folding chairs near the back of the outdoor amphitheater, off to one side, where I could not see his face. It didn't matter: I fell in love with his hands, and the back of his head. I fell in love with the sound that flowed to me when his fingers struck the keys.

I was already in love with Beethoven. I had heard this concerto as a recording many times. Last fall, a music student from my high school had played the same concerto at a local concert; I thought it sounded like he was playing scales, although I was very impressed that he could play it at all. Arnie did not sound like he was playing scales. When the concerto ended and everyone stood up and cheered and cried "Bravo," I knew I was about to meet a genius. My mother reminded me, later, that the entire audience was composed of friends and relatives of the young performers, including a fair share of Arnie's aunts and uncles and cousins, but that did not change my expectations. My father-the-music-critic decreed that he had given an outstanding performance. Not that I wanted his opinion most of the time, but now I valued it, since it confirmed mine.

After the concert was over, my parents and I were moving through the crowd with Sigrid and Ob to congratulate Arnie. I hoped my rapid heartbeat did not show through my white cotton peasant blouse. I was going to be introduced to him. My legs felt unsteady as I walked down the long aisles to the stage, where Arnie was shaking hand after hand of men and women I hoped would leave quickly. Now his friends had gathered around him, including several girls whose presence made me feel young and uncertain. One had straight long blond hair, and was smiling up at him, her head tilted at an angle I didn't trust. How well did she know him? Was she up here all summer too? Before I could speculate further, Arnie was leaving her and his group of peers to walk toward us. He had spotted his aunt and uncle.

I noted that he hugged them warmly. My family did not hug that way.

"Arnie," his Aunt Sigrid was saying, "you remember Herman and Evelyn? And have you met their daughter, Judy?" He was looking right at me as I told him how much I had enjoyed his playing. I was surprised that my voice came out sounding normal. I was more surprised when he thanked me as if he really cared what I thought. And then came the crucial question.

"Are you going to spend some time with us in Frankfort?" his aunt asked him. My heart stopped for at least a minute and a half, while he considered the invitation. "I guess I'll drive over for a day," he said. He looked directly at me when he said it. Then he smiled and said thank you and goodbye, and shook everyone's hand, including mine.

In the car on the way back, I didn't talk to anyone. I barely heard their conversation. My head was filled with sounds of Beethoven, my hand was still warm, my eyes could only see him looking at me, my body tingling. Fantasies tumbled over one another. *He would call on the phone. He would come to visit his aunt and uncle and I would open the door. Or maybe he would not call or come over; he would go directly back to Detroit. He would come over, but not be interested in talking to me. He would think I was too young. He would like me, but my mother would think he was too old for me.* While all of this was going on inside me, I sat quietly in a corner of the backseat, next to my mother and Sigrid, while they planned tomorrow's dinner. In the front seat Ob and my father, who was driving, listened to the war news on CBS radio.

When we got back to the Ruby's house in Frankfort, I went to bed, but I was too keyed up to fall asleep.

The next morning, before I had finished combing my hair, the doorbell rang.

I was closest, since I was using the mirror in the downstairs washroom, so I opened the door and there was Arnie. I was surprised to notice he was only an inch or two taller than I was. He had the broad-shouldered build of a football player, tightly curled black hair, and a face I thought was incredibly handsome: pink cheeks, full lips, clear blue eyes that were unafraid to look directly at me, and an open smile. Even though he was 19, I could see the little boy he must have been 10 years earlier.

107

After "Hi" and "Come on in" and "I liked your concert last night," I couldn't think of a thing to say. I was relieved when Aunt Sigrid appeared and invited Arnie to have some breakfast. With nine of us crowded around the breakfast table in the sunny kitchen, I didn't have to speak. We had Rice Krispies with bananas and milk, and buttered Silvercup toast, and most of the conversation was between Arnie and the adults, with Carl and Nancy interrupting a lot. I did a lot of intense staring.

After breakfast, Sigrid and the three younger kids and Arnie prepared to go down to the beach, and I went with them. I was secretly relieved that my mother could not be out in the sun and my father hated the sand and water. I put shorts and a T-shirt over my new two-piece swim suit, combed my hair, brushed my teeth for the second time and put on pale pink lipstick. I grabbed my beach towel and reached the front door just as Arnie and Carl were about to leave. The three of us walked together for the first block, and then Carl ran ahead, the pace being too slow for him. Sigrid and Nancy and Dick were already at the beach.

I had managed to think of some questions while I was combing my hair, and that made our walk more comfortable: "How did you learn that entire concerto?" and "Were you nervous playing?" and "How did you feel when the concert was over?" I was enormously relieved that he answered in paragraphs rather than monosyllables, although I could not have repeated what he said because I was thinking all the time, *Am I too young? Will he think I'm dumb? Does he like me?* and hoping I wouldn't sneeze or get the hiccups or say something stupid.

We arrived at the deep expanse of beach, and walked close to the shoreline before putting down our towels. I was delighted to notice that the group of teenagers whom I had tearfully watched through my new glasses, two summers ago, was again gathered in the center of the beach. Well, let them see me now. I was with the Prize. The Soloist. The College Man.

I no longer needed the glasses. The doctor had been wrong. My vision was 20-20 without them. And what I was seeing now was that Arnie had taken off his T-shirt and jeans, and his solid chest, back and legs were covered with dark, curly hair. Jimmy had been pale-skinned and his chest almost hairless. Arnie's masculinity turned me on even more than his piano-playing had the night before. When he asked me if I wanted to take a walk down the shoreline, I hoped my excitement didn't show. Carrying our towels, we walked north on the packed sand along the Lake Michigan shoreline, our feet cool in the water.

For some unknown reason, my ability to make intelligent conversation returned. Our conversation flowed: books, music, his relatives whom I knew, my relatives whom he knew, high school, college, his last girlfriend (also named Judy), my ex-boyfriend-as of-two-months ago, Jimmy. Younger brothers, what to do after college, and should we go back to the house and get some lunch, it's almost two o'clock.

We did. Then he left to spend some time with his family. But was I busy in the evening? No, I didn't have any other plans.

He would come by about 7:30, after dinner.

"That's nice," my mother said. "What are the two of you going to do? There is a good movie at the Bijou." She couldn't say much else: she had used his concert to lure me on this trip, he was the nephew of her hostess, and his mother was an admired acquaintance. Above all, I knew that my mother, who was already embarrassed about being a houseguest for the third time, did not want to offend anyone. But I got her message. I had seen the only movie in town three days earlier, and she knew it.

"I'm not sure. We'll see," I said vaguely.

"He's a bit old for you," she finally said. I had known that would be coming sooner or later.

"Not really," I said, and disappeared into the bathroom to study my hair again.

That evening I wore jeans and a new yellow turtleneck. It showed off my developing figure as well as anything else I could think of putting on. I was tired of buying AA bras, and had hoped to advance to at least an A cup by fall. So far, no luck.

Arnie arrived promptly at 7:30, looking like a prince in jeans and a U of M sweatshirt. He spent several minutes greeting everyone in the household. I could see that there was much affection between all of them. I waited around politely, observing his tenderness with the children, inwardly filled with impatience to get out of that house and away from everyone's (my mother's) scrutiny. Finally, having said his hellos, we both said goodbye and closed the door behind us.

He had borrowed his dad's car. We drove around aimlessly for a few minutes, and then he said, did I mind if we drove back to Interlochen, he had left some stuff there and would rather pick it up now than waste the sun tomorrow.

Did I mind? I would have driven to Nebraska if he had asked. We sang to the radio. I placed my left hand on the seat near him and he took the hint and held it when he wasn't steering around curves in the road. We stopped along the beach and watched the sun set over Lake Michigan, and then before we got back in the car, still holding hands, he stopped and kissed me. Actually, we both stopped and the kiss happened between us, very spontaneously, and it was tender and delicious, and we both felt a little unnerved by it, and got back in the car and continued driving through the dark to the camp.

Tonight the camp was empty; only a few counselors left, all the campers and parents gone. Empty and quiet. The wind whispered in the branches of the dark pines, and the scent of pine needles filled my nostrils. It was exhilarating to be here with Arnie, away from the watchful eyes of my parents and their friends. I felt special to be at Interlochen with last night's honored performer. Arnie found a flashlight in the glove compartment of the car, and guided us down a soft path between the trees to a cabin which held the things he had come for: his clothes, sheet music and some books. A young man with a mop of red hair stopped him to say hello, and he introduced us, "Larry, this is my friend Judy." *My friend. What did that mean?* I said "Hi" and then looked away, feeling suddenly awkward. *Could Larry, whoever he was, see all my feelings? Could Arnie?*

The cabin was small, warm and filled with mosquitoes. Arnie gathered his possessions quickly and I helped him carry them to the trunk of the car. We climbed into the front seat for the ride back. I sat in the middle, close to him. Before he started the motor he kissed me again and I melted into a contented silence. I had never been happier.

By the time we drove back to Frankfort it was close to ten, and I knew I should get back to the house. "I've got some stuff to do with my family in the morning," Arnie said, "but maybe we could go to the beach together after lunch." Then he parked the car, kissed me again, walked around to the other side to open the door for me, and actually came into the house with me. After all, this was his family. I couldn't believe his poise as he chatted with all the adults; I only wanted to slip away into my bedroom and relive the experience of the evening. I was afraid my emotions would glaringly show on my face. I worried that my mother would have been worried and now angry that we had driven to camp without telling her where we were going. But if she was, the presence of the others restrained her. When Arnie said goodbye to everyone, I said goodnight, walked him to the door (no kissing this time) and went directly upstairs to my room, which I shared with Nancy, to savor my good feelings.

The next morning I slept late and then lay in bed considering my extraordinary luck. I couldn't believe how different this summer was from two years ago. The more I postponed getting up, I reasoned, the shorter the time until "after lunch," the magic hour when Arnie would reappear. I also was postponing an encounter with my mother. When I finally did get up, I carefully made my bed and Nancy's and hung up yesterday's clothes before going down to breakfast. This was not the time to fuel discontent.

Everyone had finished breakfast and embarked on their morning activities. The younger kids were at the playground on the beach, the men were *schmeising* again at the card table, and Mother and Sigrid had gone grocery shopping in town. I ate some Rice Krispies, washed and dried my dish, and went out on the front porch swing to read *The Grapes of Wrath*. When the women returned from shopping, I helped them carry in the bags, put food away and make lunch. I was being the Perfect Daughter. And as long as Sigrid was with us, I was safe. Mother would never risk disapproval or embarrassment by opening up a discussion as uncomfortable as my behavior in the presence of her friend.

While we were all having lunch together, the phone rang. Ob answered it. The message was that Arnie would meet us at the beach about 2:00 o'clock. I knew the message was meant for me, and I was grateful that he had not asked to speak with me. Now I didn't have to wait in the house for a phone call and could go to the beach when the younger kids went, removing me from Mother's scrutiny. I marveled at Arnie's perceptiveness. I hoped I wasn't blushing.

When Arnie arrived at the beach, the others were in the water. I was lying on a blanket, reading. Arnie sat down next to me and I felt the sizzle of electricity between us. I was also aware that we were in view of the same group of teenagers who had always ignored me. This time there were three girls and only one boy. Compared to Arnie he looked very young. When we stood up to walk down the beach I felt tall and beautiful. One of the girls smiled in my direction. I gave her a cursory nod in return. We took our towels, found Sigrid near the shore helping Dick learn to swim, and told her we were going for a walk. Her kids were busy jumping off the pier into eight feet of water. She gave each of us a hug, said "Have a nice walk," and turned her attention back to my brother's swimming efforts.

We walked in the same direction as the day before, but this time we went farther up the coast, until we arrived at a spot where fallen trees across the shoreline made it difficult to continue. The beach was very narrow here, backed by woods, and the lake bottom filled with small rocks. It was a good place to stop. We put our towels over the trunk of a large tree, on a spot where the bark had fallen away and the wood was smooth. It made a comfortable bench. Arnie was talkative and I, trained to listen to my father, was a willing audience. He was knowledgeable about literature and theater as well as music. He told me about some of his music teachers and about classes he had taken the previous semester. When we tired of sitting on the log we stood up and skipped stones across the surface of the lake. We found sticks and wrote our names in the sand and watched as the water washed them away.

And then it was late in the afternoon, and time to return.

"I'll come over about 8:00," Arnie said. "Maybe we can go to the new movie at the Bijou." I liked that he didn't have to ask; he just knew.

"Come home early," Mother said as we left. "We will," Arnie promised. I was silent.

"Do you want to go to the show?" Arnie asked me when we were out the door. I grinned and shook my head. "Good" he said. "I know a nice stretch of beach where we can watch the end of the sunset." We climbed into his car, drove about ten minutes south of town, and parked near the beach. Arnie took a blanket and flashlight out of the trunk of the car. We walked through a grove of trees, the sky ahead of us turning a deep pink.

"Just in time for the grand finale," he said. He spread out the blanket between a large tree and the beach, so that he could lean against the tree while I leaned against him, and we sat watching the sky perform its dance of colors for us. The air felt soft against my face, though it was growing cool. I was glad I had pulled a sweatshirt over my short-sleeved T-shirt. White gulls were circling, seeking their final meal of the day. Water lapped musically over the sand, leaving bubbles of white foam. We listened to the song of cicadas and bass tones of a frog. Before us a painting was being created, the invisible brush sweeping the sky, spreading splashes of orange and pink, then erasing those to add deeper tones of magenta.

My back was against his chest, his arms clasped around me somewhere above my waist but not too high. I could feel his breath warm against my right ear. I wanted to hold this moment forever.

When the curtain fell over the sky and it grew dark, the stars began to emerge, one at a time, and the 3/4 moon glowed above us. I turned, so that I was leaning across him, and he held me, and then we were kissing. And kissing. I had kissed other boys, and had necked with Jimmy often, but this was different. This was Arnie playing the Emperor Concerto. Each kiss was distinct, the way each note speaks when played by a master musician. The music of Beethoven soared through my body.

There was no grand climax to this crescendo. I was too young and the social mores and sexual taboos of 1948 were far too strong for that. A few brushes of the hand between the sweatshirt, and the T-shirt, in the area of the AA bra. It was enough.

I thought I could have gone on kissing him forever, except that my lips were beginning to feel sore and I was trying hard not to sneeze. Suddenly Arnie glanced at his glow-in-the-dark watch and said softly, "Uh-oh—it's after 11:00 and your mom wanted you back early." We stood up stiffly, stretched, shook out the blanket, folded it and walked through the dark to the car, holding hands in silence. I was in a strange state of arousal mixed with sadness: I knew that Arnie was leaving for Detroit in the morning. Anxiety was there, too; I prayed that no one would be waiting up to ask where I had been. Added to this mixture, the night air had begun to activate my hay fever. The attack arrived suddenly and with force. I sneezed unromantically most of the way home.

As we drove, hands still touching, I felt a question burning inside me. I was afraid but I felt compelled to ask. Somehow I gathered the courage.

"Arnie," I said. "I have to know something. All this, yesterday and today, did it mean anything to you? Or was it just...a summer thing?"

There. It was out. I could hardly believe I had put him on the spot like that and taken such a risk myself. But I had to know.

He paused, trying to choose his words carefully. But there was no way to do that. "I guess it was just summer," he said.

It felt like a miracle of strength that I was able to withhold my tears, to say "Thanks for being honest with me," and "It's been very special." I added, "Please don't walk me to the door," and got into the house before the flood broke. Miraculously, the house was quiet. A light had been left on for me in the hallway that led to the staircase. I turned it out when I reached the top. Nancy and I shared a room; because I couldn't risk waking her up, I went into the bathroom, shut the door, flushed the toilet and cried loudly while it was making noise. Then I locked the bathroom door, curled up on the rug and sobbed, trying to muffle the sound with a bath towel.

These were not light tears falling. It was impossible to cry quietly, as I had done many times in my life, weeping softly into a pillow with no sound. This was a storm. My body felt torn apart as I gave way to wrenching sobs. Finally, exhausted, I crawled off the floor and into my bed, to sleep until morning.

In the morning my period started, and I used that as an excuse not to come down to breakfast. I didn't want to face him if he came to say goodbye to everyone, which he did. "Tell him I'm still asleep," I begged my Mother, when she came upstairs to rouse me. "I've got cramps." I knew she would never tell him that; she would be too embarrassed.

So everyone else ate breakfast, and I stayed in bed, bleeding, crampy, and feeling like my insides had been cut by knives, alternately sneezing, crying, and dozing off, until just before noon, when Mother came up to the bedroom with a cup of tea for me, with honey, the way she knew I liked it.

"Arnie said to say goodbye to you," she said. "He seemed disappointed not to see you. He said to tell you he'll call you when we're back in Detroit."

She patted my cheek. "Why don't you get up and wash your face," she said, "and maybe we'll go shopping for something new for school."

"And, dear," she added, just before she left to go downstairs, "I think he really is too old for you."

On her coffee table, Sigrid had a 3x5 black and white photo of Arnie on the beach; before we left for home, she gave it to me to keep. He's crouching in the sand like a football player, his furry chest bare and his beautiful face smiling into the camera. I slept with it under my pillow. *"He looked disappointed" my mother had said. "He said he'd call you."* When school began, I showed his picture to my girlfriends. "This is the guy I went out with this summer. He goes to U. of M." For my girlfriends in the music depart-ment at Cass Tech, I added, "He won a contest at Interlochen and played the Emperor Concerto." They were impressed.

Lots of boys asked me out on dates early that fall, now that Jimmy was out of the picture. I went out and had fun but I waited for that call from Arnie. The sharp pain had subsided and warm memories remained. Finally, in late September, the call came. He was coming home from Ann Arbor in two weeks. "I have two tickets for *A Midsummer Night's Dream* at Wayne University," he said. "Do you want to go with me?"

For days before, I agonized over what to wear. I had a nice pleated skirt and cashmere sweater, but saddle shoes did not seem appropriate. Mother took me shopping and I found a pair of black suede low wedgies that tied around the ankle. That problem taken care of, I worried about understand-ing Shakespeare.

The date with Arnie felt more formal than being at the beach. He wore a suit and tie, in the style of the day. Once again, like the first time I met him, I found conversation awkward. I couldn't think of a single topic to initiate, or even any questions to get him going. During the play, this was not an issue. But I had difficulty following the story and the language, and so did not enjoy it fully. Fearing I would sound stupid or rude, I didn't want to admit this to him. After the play, as was the local custom of the decade, he took me out to eat. We went to a deli that was not far from where I lived. As we ate our corned beef sandwiches, I didn't feel any of the summer chemistry between us and felt brain-dead as we strained to make conversation.

Walking in the dark from the deli to the side street where Arnie's car was parked, we had to cross an alley. Houses and businesses in Detroit all had alleys behind their property. The alleys crossed over the sidewalks, end-ing at the street. Even as late as 1948, "junkmen" still traveled with horse and wagon through those alleys to collect rags, old clothes, bottles and newspapers. Their horses did not wear little bags to catch their waste, as do modern-day horses near Central Park in NY. In the dark, crossing the alley near the car, I stepped in a piece of what a horse had dropped.

At first, I only knew by the slippery feeling on the bottom of my shoe. Arnie didn't see it happen, and I was too drop-dead embarrassed to say any-thing. I tried to inconspicuously scrape it off on the curb when Arnie was on the other side of the car. As we got into his car, I could smell the odor rising. Neither of us mentioned anything about it. Fortunately, the ride home only lasted for a few blocks. At my door, standing on the downstairs porch, Arnie said goodnight and gave me a perfunctory kiss. He didn't say, "I'll call you." We thanked each other for a nice evening and he left. I took off my new shoes, wrapped them in a paper bag and threw them in the garbage.

Fast Forward...

I didn't see Arnie again until after I had finished college and was married to Bob, perhaps ten years later. For some reason I can't recall, he was driving his car with my cousin Carolyn in the front seat; Bob and I were in the back. It must have been transportation that Carolyn's mother, my Aunt Sunny, who was a friend of Arnie's relatives, had arranged to some mutual event, perhaps a wedding. I was dressed up and felt particularly glowing that day.

I noticed changes in him. He had gained weight, looking more rotund like his father and uncles. His thick curly hair was receding. He told us he no longer played the piano seriously, and had gone to work in the family furniture business. He had not married. His smile was the same, and his eyes. When he saw me, his face expressed astonishment, delight and, I thought, something like regret.

It was, I report with chagrin, a satisfying encounter.

Cass Technical High School

❧

When it was time to enroll in high school, my parents were concerned about where I would attend. Detroit was divided into school districts. We lived between two of them. To the north was Central, where most of the Jewish kids went. To the south was Northwestern, my official district, with a growing population of "coloreds." Some Jewish kids I knew gave false addresses, such as a grandparent's, so they could go to Central. My parents did not approve of doing that since it was illegal. Besides, my father had worked hard to be assimilated and was not eager for me to go to Central.

"Forget Central," he said. "We're not giving any false addresses."

My mother, however, was not comfortable about sending me to Northwestern.

"It's not a very good neighborhood," was how she put it. I knew what she really meant. Although she had always taught me that all people are equal and deserved equal opportunities, when it came right down to it, she was unwilling to send me to school with so many Negroes.

Like most decisions in my life at that time, I had little to say, and waited for my parents to solve the dilemma.

One day my father came home and announced that he had just talked with his old friend, William Stirton, who was the Principal at Cass Technical High School. Cass was located almost downtown but was unique in being both a neighborhood school and an all-city one, drawing top students to its many special departments. "Bill" urged my father to send me to Cass. Because I was a student with good grades, he was sure I would fit in nicely. The school was divided into specialized curriculums and my father had brought home a book explaining each one. My mother was excited at the idea of this alternative, and even I was intrigued. All we had to do was pick a curriculum.

We sat around the dining table going through the book together. First we eliminated all the departments that were mostly for boys: architectural drafting, mechanical drawing and auto mechanics. Then we studied the more cultural/intellectual departments: art, music and science. I felt totally unqualified for each of these. Despite six years of violin lessons, I could not read the notes above first position, which meant I could not play in the school orchestra. I had no artistic talents and was totally disinterested in science.

There was not much left other than pre-nursing and home economics. Pre-nursing was out: Jewish girls did not become nurses. That left home economics, which consisted of classes in cooking, sewing and nutrition. It sounded pretty boring. But my mother made a good case for learning what she considered life skills and my father was happy that I could be at Cass, with any curriculum. The matter was decided. I would go to Cass Tech and major in home economics.

To get there I had to take two busses, early in the morning. Because I had never been allowed to travel the city much by myself, this was very exciting. Another girl from my former intermediate school home room, Shirley, lived on the way to the first bus stop and we went together. We took the 14th Street bus to West Grand Boulevard and then transferred to a bus that went downtown, stopping near Cass on the way. That first fall, the bus ride was an adventure: leaving home alone when it was barely light outside and stopping for Shirley. She was a very bright, well-built Jewish girl who, in 9th grade, had won the all-city forensics contest, sponsored by the Daughters of the American Revolution, with a speech about European immigrants entering the United States. We had been only casual friends at Hutchins, but she seemed happy to see me each morning and I felt less alone.

The building that housed the school occupied an entire square block. There were eight floors, and elevators, although it was usually quicker to walk up and down the broad staircases than to wait for a slow elevator. The halls were noisy and mobbed with students. It was confusing at first but also exhilarating.

The home economics classrooms were equipped: some had stoves with ovens; others had sewing machines. In cooking class we learned how to cut butter into flour with two knives in preparation for making baking powder biscuits and how to make cream sauce for creamed chipped beef on toast. In sewing class I learned how to make a flat-felled seam down the legs of pajama pants. I also made a blouse and a dress which I hated. I never put any of the cooking skills to use, nor did I wear any of the clothes I made.

What I learned from being in home ec (as we called it) was more interesting than the intended curriculum. The other girls were from backgrounds totally different from my own. I learned things about other lives that I never would have known outside of novels. My closest home ec friend was Mavis. Her mother had died, her father was in a home for alcoholics in California, and she lived with her married older sister. Her sister's husband had done sexual things to her. She told me her stories while we were measuring ingredients for baking powder biscuits. Once I visited her at her sister's home. The sister, an aunt and the aunt's daughter were all in the backyard, talking. Each of them had her hair in rollers, although it was 2:00 pm and they weren't going anywhere that evening. The aunt asked me if my family was in the pickle business, because she bought a brand at the corner grocery called "Judy's Pickles." I thought she was joking, but it was actually a serious question.

Another girl who sat near Mavis and me in cooking class was Mary, a thin, pale child who looked younger than her 13 years. Her father was in the Merchant Marines and was out to sea most of the time. Her mother raised the five children alone until he came home and began barking out orders. If I didn't learn anything useful about cooking, sewing or nutrition, I received many lessons in sociology.

The teacher I recall most vividly was a thin woman with yellow-white hair and a stooped posture, who taught all three subjects (cooking, sewing and nutrition) and who seemed to like me more than I liked her. Her name was Birdie Considine, and I thought she looked a bit like a bird, with her thin arms and delicate features. Other girls were afraid of her, because she was quite a strict disciplinarian, but I wasn't afraid—only bored by the things we had to do, like charting everything we ate during the day (nutrition class) or making white cream sauce. My mother, an excellent cook, never made cream sauce, especially over meat. Her mother had kept kosher; kosher Jews never ate meat and milk at the same meal, never mind in the same recipe.

My closest friends at Cass Tech were Jewish girls in the art and music departments. My new friend Gloria, in music, had a beautiful singing voice, and an Italian boyfriend who played trumpet. He was deeply in love with her; when she went to the University of Michigan and broke up with him, his heart was broken. He played with the Detroit Symphony for years but never married. She married a Jewish doctor.

Another friend, Connie, a redhead, was good natured, feisty and also a very talented artist. We hung out together a lot after school and on weekends. (Most kids assumed I was in the art department, which had more status than home economics, and often I let them think that.) I was less close with Connie's girlfriend Joanne, another red-headed artist, but half a grade ahead of us. They lived on the same block. Years later, Joanne and I became closer friends when we were married and had little boys of similar ages. Still later, she designed the cover for my first published volume of poems.

Sara Ann was another highly creative student in the art department. We remained friends for a lifetime, even after she married and moved to California. Her son, Max, and grandson, Ari, have remained special people in my life even after Sara's death in 2007.

What I loved most about Cass Tech was my independence. Until then, my life had been spent close to home, monitored carefully by my mother. At Cass I felt free of such close scrutiny. I joined the newspaper staff and several school clubs, and had a wide spectrum of friends. I "belonged." I walked with friends after school to downtown Detroit, enjoying the spring air, the safety of the streets, and the wonderful department stores.

In my senior year I tried out for a part in the school play. I was given the part of Mother in "Mother was a Freshman," a story about a woman who goes to college while her daughter is in high school. In the late 1940's, that was a very *avant garde* theme. The role of my daughter was played by my childhood friend, Lois Karbel, who loved acting and performed with ease. In one scene I had to twirl across the stage, happily. I couldn't twirl: I was too stiff and inhibited. Lois spent hours trying to teach me. We rehearsed this little play from October until May, during and after school, until the entire cast was sick of it. Rehearsing for so long and having only one performance was ridiculous. The teacher in charge was reported to be alcoholic and sometimes did not show up for after-school rehearsals.

As the evening of our sole performance approached, I became increasingly anxious. The afternoon before our evening show, I was so nervous I felt physically ill. I did not want to be in that play! I spent the day at Connie's house, telling her that I understood why people had the urge to walk in front of a bus. I was ready to fake breaking a leg to get out of being in that play. Ultimately, I did my part, with my family watching, and was overcome with relief when it was over. That was the beginning and the end of my career as an actress.

Despite the play, my three years at Cass Tech provided many positive experiences. High school gave me time to grow out of childhood and into a more confident person. It also was a legitimate escape from the troubles brewing at home.

Being Jewish: High School

When I was in high school and starting to go out with boys, my mother made it very clear that they had to be Jewish. This was not unusual for those times, although it did not make much sense to me. The first boy I had a crush on in high school was Greek. He was on the basketball team, and let me wear his letter-sweater. He could not go out with me, either, because I wasn't Greek. In fact, his parents had already arranged a marriage for him with the daughter of friends of theirs. She was two years older than he was and he had no interest in her at all. But he understood my mother's rule, so we simply remained good friends in school.

In the 11th grade, although I was dating many different Jewish boys, I was obsessed with Bill, a boy in my school whose parents were German Catholic. He had curly blond hair and sensitive blue eyes; he was intelligent and a fine visual artist. I thought about him day and night. I don't think that Bill had started dating yet, and I know that he had no extra spending money for dates. We didn't go out formally, but after school was over, we used to walk downtown from Cass Technical High School to the J.L. Hudson Company Department Store. There we took an elevator to the 13th floor music store. We both loved classical music, and Hudson's provided booths where people could sit quietly to preview recordings before purchasing them. We sat together in our private booth, sharing our favorite pieces with each other. Sometimes we listened to several versions of the same piece, perhaps a violin concerto played by different artists, and discussed the differences in style and performance. We listened for hours but never bought anything.

One night I went with Bill and a group of friends to a school concert. Afterward we all went out to eat at a busy restaurant near the school. The juke box played *There was a boy, a very strange enchanted boy. . .* To this day, whenever I hear that song from 1948, I remember the magic of that boy and that evening. We had to wait quite a while for a table. I always went out to eat as part of a weekend date, so, although this was a school night, it did not occur to me to call home to say I would be late.

When the car's driver finally deposited me at my front door, my mother was in the window, waiting. She had been worried, and it came out in a torrent of rage, including the words, "You are never going to see that boy again. He isn't even Jewish!"

After such a wonderful evening (I sat on Bill's lap in the overcrowded back seat, and kissed him for the first time) I was totally devastated. I sobbed into my pillow all night and woke up in grief the next morning. Whatever my mother was trying to convey had the opposite effect: I knew I would never place such a limiting religious restriction on my own children.

My friend Sara Ann invited me to a Friday night gathering of a Jewish group called *Habonim*. The boys and girls whom I met that night, and on subsequent Fridays, were very smart, loved classical music, Hebrew songs and Jewish circle dancing, and were ardent Zionists. I had never met such a fun group before. The girls didn't wear makeup and some didn't shave their legs. These kids were non-pretentious and committed to their ideals.

My parents were not Zionists, and, in 1947, at age 14, I knew almost nothing about the issues of building a new Jewish state, or whether it would be good or bad for the Jews. I don't think I cared too much one way or another. I was there because I loved the singing and dancing, the camaraderie and intellectual banter. In the summer, when my new friends went to Habonim Camp, part of the Labor Zionist youth organization, I did not press my parents to send me. I knew they would say no; beyond that, I didn't share or even understand my friends' passion for Zionism. Even in this very friendly, accepting Jewish group, I felt once again at the edge.

❧

In 10th grade, I decided to rejoin the Sunday school program I had left many years earlier at Temple Beth El. I wanted to learn more about Judaism and I also wanted to increase my social contacts with other Jewish kids. I wanted to belong somewhere. My mother was very happy with this decision; my father, indifferent. What I learned about Judaism was negligible. I was more involved with the social contacts. I made some new girlfriends and, once I had finally broken up with Jimmy, at the end of 10th grade, met many new boys to date.

In 12th grade, a local attorney taught an excellent class in Comparative Religion. Each student picked a religion to study and we presented our findings to the class. I selected Baha'i, which turned out to be a fortuitous choice when, many years later, a Protestant daughter-in-law and three of our grandchildren joined a Baha'i group. I had some background in what they were doing and a positive attitude.

∾

Just before I graduated from high school, my father was suddenly and inexplicably fired from the auto industry public relations job he had held for many years. His boss, the top man at AMA, had retired; the man who took over gave my father's position to someone else. My father was in shock. His closest friend at work, a man highly admired by everyone in the organization, investigated. Within a short time he told my father what he had learned.

"Herman, you were the only Jew in the office," Christy said. "It was out- and-out anti-Semitism."

As later became public knowledge, the Detroit auto industry was rife with anti-Semitism, from the top levels down. At the time, however, most of the general public was unaware, and my educated, assimilated father most of all. His level of denial, his feeling that "This doesn't apply to me," prevented him from recognizing what surrounded him until it was too late.

My family was now in a difficult financial bind, needing to move and looking for a new house. In addition, I was about to enroll in freshman classes at Detroit's Wayne University, not yet a State school in 1950. I went to the scholarship office to see if they would help me with tuition. I was nervous and embarrassed. The woman who interviewed me at the Financial Aid office was more hostile than empathic. She fired many questions at me about my family.

"Why do you think you need aid?"

"My father lost his job."

"Why do you think he was fired?"

"Because he was Jewish," I blurted naively.

The woman stared at me, in shock. "That's a terrible accusation! You have no way of knowing that. You should never say such a thing without proof."

"His Gentile friend, who still works there, found out. *He* told us that. My father was the only Jewish person working there," I said.

"Well, we'll consider your request and let you know," she said, dismissing me.

I was eventually granted a tuition scholarship. My satisfaction at this news was overpowered by my regret that I had spoken honestly. Worse, I remember my deep discomfort at having to admit to this non-empathic woman that I was Jewish.

A Walk with my Father

❧

The winter of my senior year in high school, just before my 17th birthday and many months before my encounter with the financial aid woman at Wayne University, the two-family flat where we had rented for thirteen years was sold. This meant that the nice older couple who lived downstairs would be leaving and the new owners moving in. My mother seemed both apprehensive and excited.

"They're from Kentucky," she told me dubiously. "And they may want our flat for their relatives to move into." She frowned. Then she smiled. "But maybe this will be our chance to move. Something nice, that's just our own. Not rented."

My parents had always been friendly with the downstairs neighbors, and in earlier years, when children my age lived there, I enjoyed having another place to play. But now that I was a senior, and privately mourning the loss of Bill, the boy I'd been obsessed with who had graduated last June, I didn't care much about who lived where. My thoughts were totally inward, my energy depleted by longing. I listened to my mother as if from the other side of a glass wall. What did it mean to me if they were from Kentucky? Who cared?

When the new landlords moved in, the entire feeling of the house changed. The shared entrance hall smelled. It had never smelled before. It was an unpleasant odor that I could not identify. "Cabbage and pork and dog poop," my mother said in disgust. The hallway was also dirty. Previously, whoever lived downstairs took care of sweeping up the dust, wiping off the melted snow. Now it was never cleaned. Sheets from old newspapers littered the floor. Once, a piece of an old rubber tire was left outside their door. It became increasingly unpleasant to come home. "Hillbillies," my mother said. She had always lectured me about tolerance, and I was shocked to hear this side of her come out.

I had just come home from school one day, my arms full of books, and was changing out of my plaid wool skirt and cashmere sweater into a pair of jeans and my father's old shirt, when Mother knocked on my door. My stomach clenched automatically: what had I done that she was angry about? Nothing, it turned out. Mother had news. "Those new owners downstairs," (she never called them by name; I'm not sure if I ever knew their names) "those people want their cousins from Kentucky to take our flat. Our lease is up in August; we'll have to move." She was crying. I wanted to hug her, but we didn't do that, my mother and I, so I walked over and touched her arm. I was totally at a loss for what to say to comfort her. Making her feel better was the only thought in my mind. It did not occur to me to have an opinion or a feeling of my own about moving.

"Maybe now you can buy the house you've always wanted," I tried, feeling tentative.

"I'm not sure we have enough money saved," she said, "but I think we can do it." Then she changed from the one needing comfort back into my mother, the one I expected when the knock came. "Hang up your clothes. Look at that nice skirt; it's going to wrinkle on the bed like that." I had just taken it off seconds before she knocked, but I knew better than to argue. "We spend money to get you nice things and you don't even take care of them." Her voice was rising. I picked up the skirt and hung it carefully on a skirt hanger. Mother's face softened; I knew she was sorry and I knew she was unable to tell me. She left for the kitchen and I closed my door and tried unsuccessfully to concentrate on my homework.

For as long as I could recall, my parents had talked of the safety of renting over the risk of buying. Each set of grandparents had purchased homes in the late '20s only to lose them in the Great Depression, a time which felt as irrelevant to me as the Civil War history I was learning in school. My father had vowed never to get into the same situation. So he had paid his monthly rent for over twenty years, and now, in the early months of 1950, he had no equity and soon would have no place to live. With limited choice, however, he joined my mother in conversation about which part of the city they should look at, what kind of house, and on Sundays took her for rides to look at possible neighborhoods.

Whenever I emerged from my own inner world of current dates and former crushes, and paid attention to my household, I noticed that my father had once again become withdrawn. After work he sat down with his newspaper, didn't speak at dinner except to snap at my brother (who, as far as I could see, was not doing anything wrong) and after dinner he took his nap on the living room sofa. By that time I had retreated to my bedroom, after helping mother with the dishes. I had long since stopped asking him to look at my homework, particularly if it involved writing, because he edited it until it was his, not mine. I learned I could pull an A by myself. So we had little interaction. I missed the Daddy who had been openly talkative, because I enjoyed the contact of being his audience. I waited for him to return.

One Saturday in early spring, when Mother was out with a friend, my father asked me to go for a walk with him. "I need to talk to you about something." he said. This felt ominous but intriguing. It was not an invitation: it was both a plea and an order. I never said *No* to my father: not out of fear, as with my mother, but because his commanding presence did not leave room for insubordination. He seldom controlled my choice of activities, leaving that realm to my mother. She was the one who waited up in the living room, face grim, until I came home from a date at 1:30 in the morning; he went to sleep. His realm of control had to do with neatness: *Put all the pencils back where they belong; make sure the boots are lined up in the closet properly; hang up your coat straight, not falling off the hanger; don't leave your book lying open on the couch: put in a book mark and put it back on the shelf.* The list went on. They were not difficult matters for me to comply with, although it may have been another story for my brother, who was continually being scolded for something or other.

We walked and I listened. My father's pace was slower than usual, his forehead in deep furrows. "I don't want to tell your mother this yet," he said. "I don't want to upset her unnecessarily. I've lost my job as of the end of July. But I'm sure I'll have a new one by August. I have lots of leads."

Then he took my hand.

It was that gesture, not the news of job loss, which put me into shock. My father needed me. He trusted me. He was upset. He wanted me to comfort him. I was important. I was loved. He thought I could handle this better than my mother could. I was no longer just a stupid child in his eyes.

129

His hand felt familiar, the same hand I had held all through my childhood crossing streets. His palms were soft and uncalloused, the hands of a man who read, wrote, did no manual work. The backs were hairy, veined. This time I did not feel like a little girl holding daddy's hand. He was asking me for something; I was to be the adult. As familiar as his hand felt, the situation felt that strange. Holding his hand on an afternoon in April, walking down the sidewalk of our street, past the houses of people we knew, felt unnatural. I held hands with boys on dates; this was different.

The leaves on the hedges between each house had emerged from the bud-like stage they had been in the last time I walked here. They were not quite the full size they would reach by summer, but close to it. How had that happened so quickly, so invisibly? I had watched the buds every year, walking to school, or, when I was in high school, to the bus stop. I decided long ago that they must grow at night, when I was asleep.

"How can we buy a house?" I asked him.

"Don't worry, don't worry, it's all taken care of," he said. But now, for the first time in my life, I didn't believe him.

"Daddy, how can you take Mom to look for houses and not tell her about your job?" I was confused. I had never been given any information about household decisions or finances. That belonged to the category of "certain things children don't need to know." But I sensed that something was very wrong here.

"Oh, Judy, I'm so scared," he said. It was the most uncharacteristic statement I had ever heard from my father. His words felt like the stab of a knife through my body. He was scared, he was losing a job, my mother was excitedly looking for a new house, her dream house, we had no choice about moving less than two months after I would graduate from high school, and I was being asked to keep this major secret from my mother. I was used to keeping secrets from my mother, but they were my own secrets. I felt queasy.

"Why are you losing your job?" I finally thought to ask.

"I don't know, I don't know." He brushed it aside with a characteristic gesture, a wave of the hand, a motion that usually meant, "Don't ask foolish questions," but I knew it meant that he could really not explain it.

"They have a new boss; he's letting me go and replacing me with his friend." He shook his head. "It doesn't make any sense."

I squeezed his hand. We walked a while in silence. I didn't know what else to ask and I had no advice to offer. I was totally ignorant of the world of jobs and money; my father had taken care of all of us, my mother included. He was the take-charge person. He did the driving, not only metaphorically but literally. He had discouraged my mother in her wish to learn to drive, and she had never learned. I had taken driver's training in school, but he never once had let me practice in his car. He let no one, even his brothers, drive his car. He would rather give me an allowance than have me work or baby sit for my own money. He even set my alarm clock every night, rather than risk having me doing it incorrectly. I didn't know how to respond to this new father, the one asking for support.

We had turned back toward our house. There were puddles on the sidewalk where the pavement sloped inward. We were both careful to avoid them. My father's legendary caution would not allow him to get his shoes wet. He would be even more upset if I stepped in the water, and I didn't want to upset him any further.

As we reached our driveway, he let go of my hand and straightened his posture. "Just don't tell your mother any of this. We'll find a house and I'll have a new job before we have to close on it. This is just temporary."

My mother could be explosive and my father could not tolerate this trait in her without becoming angry. I could not bear either her explosions or his anger. I had always been taught not to reveal anyone's secrets. All of that made it easy for me to agree to my father's request. However, I also had been taught all my life not to lie. My father had always said, "One lie leads to another to cover it up, and then another, and pretty soon you're in a web you can't get out of." Now I had a dilemma: it was forbidden to lie, and forbidden to reveal a secret. Was failing to speak the same as lying? Would I be lying to my mother by letting her buy a house I knew my father might not be able to afford? Was I protecting her, or betraying her? It was too much for me to figure out.

We walked up the four steps to the outer porch. My father turned his key in the lock of the heavy outer door that led into the shared downstairs hallway. Ahead of us was the stairway to our flat with its familiar black rubber tread. I wanted to run upstairs and hide in my bedroom, but I didn't. I waited for my father. He walked very slowly, tightly gripping the polished mahogany banister.

Mother was waiting at the top of the stairs. I couldn't look directly at her. I said, "Hi," and squeezed past, leaving her to take care of my father. As I reached my bedroom I heard her say, "I wish you would just snap out of this, Herman," and his reply: "You don't understand, dear. You just don't understand."

After Graduation

I spent the rest of the summer in the glow of a New Boyfriend, purposely detached from the events in my household, while my parents drove around the northwest section of Detroit looking at houses, my mother still not knowing my father was without a job. Eventually they found a place my mother loved, in the newer northwest section of the city, where many of her friends lived. "It's like a little doll house," she said excitedly, "and it's in perfect condition to move into." I remained aloof from this drama, riding my bike to friends' houses nearby, including that of the New Boyfriend. That created additional tension between my mother and me: she thought it inappropriate for a girl to go to a boy's house.

At some point my father must have confessed the situation to my mother. As was the case in my family, this revelation, as well as details of moving and house payments, was not discussed in front of me. I later learned that a friend of my father loaned him the cash to buy the house. My mother proceeded to organize the rooms, but her joy was gone. She felt humiliation at having to borrow, anger at my father and a feeling of betrayal. I never knew if she suspected that my father had confided in me. In typical fashion for my family, nothing was openly discussed.

My father had become even more anxious and depressed. Someone had the good sense to get him to a psychiatrist, where he received medication. Then, after several months, he suddenly bounded out of depression into a stream of non-stop cheerful talking. The exhortation to "Just snap out if it, Herman!" was replaced by "Stop talking, Herman!" and sometimes, in exasperation, "Shut up, Herman!" Eventually someone found him a job, which he was unready to handle, and there followed several years of other short-term jobs he disliked, along with more episodes of manic-depressive illness (the term "bi-polar" was not yet in our vocabulary in 1950) and one or two lengthy psychiatric hospitalizations.

When fall arrived, the New Boyfriend moved out of state to his new job, and I began college at Wayne University, taking a bus to school every day. It was a time of tension and unhappiness for my parents and the beginning of a new adventure for me.

College

∾

Attending Wayne and Meeting Bob

In my limited world of Jewish friends, when you graduated from high school it was a given that you went to college. Choosing a college was not the two-year process in those days that it has since become. It was simple: there were only two choices of which I was aware, Wayne University, in the heart of Detroit, or the more prestigious University of Michigan, in Ann Arbor, a two-hour car ride away, necessitating room and board. The choice was determined by family income. In my case, for financial reasons, U of M was not a consideration.

At first I thought that going to Wayne would be much like going to Cass Tech, except that I would take one long bus ride instead of two short ones. To my surprise, and delight, I soon discovered that I had entered a realm of mind-opening courses and dynamic professors.

The physical site of Wayne in 1950 was primitive by today's standards of campuses and architecture. When I enrolled, World War II was only six years past and new construction was just beginning. Many of my classes were held in Quonset huts, temporary metal structures left over from the war years. They were cold in the winter and hot in the summer, but they served to house the growing number of students, including returning war veterans who were flocking in, their tuition covered by the GI Bill. The only substantial-looking building was Old Main, a three-story red brick, ivy covered structure on Cass Avenue at Warren, built in 1896. It had once been the old Central High School, which my mother had attended. During my undergraduate years, the Science Building and State Hall were added. There was no real campus. Cars passed freely along city streets that were not yet closed to traffic.

I was less interested in the architecture than in managing to get from one building to another within the ten minutes allotted between classes. It was the content of those classes and the high quality of the instruction that opened my mind to the world. For the most part, all my undergraduate classes were taught by full professors of the highest caliber. I was an English major, and the professors were so far above anything I had ever experienced that I can still recall their lectures today, six decades later.

Orville Linck taught Introduction to World Literature. We read everything from *Agamemnon* to *The Cherry Orchard*; from *Huckleberry Finn* to T.S. Eliot. Dr. Linck read passages aloud in his booming voice and I was thrilled. He elaborated on literary devices and ethical issues. He made us think. One day I shyly asked if he would look at some poems I had written. Even though this was not a writing class, he made an appointment to see me in his office and was highly encouraging. He suggested I contact the poetry editor of *Panorama*, the student literary magazine. I did, and became an assistant poetry editor, with my name on the masthead and my poems in the journal. I was too new to this world to recognize the honor, and regret I didn't save those issues.

Shakespeare class was taught by Dr. Leo Kirschbaum, a Shakespeare scholar with a national reputation. We spent an entire semester, from September to January, on *Othello*, barely finishing Act One. I have kept a deep appreciation for the multitude of nuances in each line of Shakespeare's plays and how the choice of the many possible interpretations shapes the meaning of the play.

I still remember the faces and teaching styles, if not all the names, of my professors as well as the content of my English classes. In American Literature, I recognized for the first time how literature and history intertwined. In high school, they simply had been separate classes and I never saw the connection. Also in American Literature, I was intrigued by the religious or spiritual philosophies of Transcendentalism, Pantheism and Deism, as addressed in the writings of some of the founders of our country. Reading non-biblical perspectives on the nature of God and the universe triggered a longing in me to understand more. I didn't know what I believed but I was glad to learn there were more than two choices (the traditional God-in-the-sky, or atheism). My spiritual longing remained with me, active though underground, not pursued for many years.

In a course in the 19th and 20th century novel, Woodburn Ross had us reading a novel a week, a hefty assignment along with my other homework. One of the books about which I had to write a paper was *Heart of Darkness*, by Joseph Conrad. I was out of my depth; I simply lacked the maturity to understand the philosophy. I wrote a paper extolling Conrad for his exceptionally beautiful prose style, his depth of philosophical thought and the action of the plot. Ross wrote on my paper, "You write beautifully without really saying anything." B minus. I wasn't sure whether to feel complimented or slapped, but I knew he had me pegged correctly.

Another eye-opening class was Victorian Literature: James McCormick went through each line of poetry word by word, explaining so that the poems made sense and came to life. Having so recently begun to write poetry myself, I drank in every word.

Wonderful outsiders, not quite famous but on their way, were brought in to speak or give poetry readings. Dylan Thomas read his poems in a State Hall lecture room in the 1950's; and in the '60's, Seamus Heaney, still relatively unknown, read also in his wonderful Irish brogue, seated at a desk in a small classroom.

The History Department was equally outstanding. Dr. Milton Covensky's class in World History was one of the most popular on the campus. He taught with the door to the room open so that anyone passing by could come in; his voice and our laughter drew a standing-room-only audience.

"Put your pencils down," he would admonish us, "and just listen. I'll dictate notes to study for the test, later." We listened with rapt attention.

"What do civilizations do?" he asked at the start of every class, to which we replied in unison, "They rise, mature and decline." Dr. Covensky moved his arms in illustration; he was a conductor leading the chorus. Some of us began to suspect that the United States might not be invincible forever.

"Where did the Greeks keep their women?" he would ask daily.

"In the back room," was our shouted answer. In this way he taught us about sexism in ancient Greece and we remembered.

❦

Ask any Jewish woman of my cohort what their mothers told them to study and the answer is the same. "Be a teacher," they all said. "You can always get a job and even if you get married, you can always fall back on it." (They meant, *Even if your husband can't support you or you get divorced or, God forbid, he dies...*) Dutifully, we all became teachers. And years later, when teaching jobs were scarce and our mothers turned out to have been wrong, many of us turned to social work or psychology and became therapists.

I had become too much of an intellectual snob to major in the College of Education classes that had the reputation of being "Mickey Mouse," so I stayed in Liberal Arts as an English major and took enough courses in Secondary Education to be certified to teach grades 7-12 after graduation.

∾

Class work was important, but so were relationships. Two happened in 1950, my freshman year, and have continued throughout my life. I met Adelle, who became my best friend. We felt a perfect rapport. We took most of our classes together, spent hours at each other's houses (mostly at hers, because she lived closer to school), double-dated, shared secrets, laughed a lot, and often finished each other's sentences, or spoke the same words at the same time. Our attunement was a delight for both of us. We spent time together daily for three years, until she married and moved east to New Haven, Connecticut, where her husband, Bob Rosenzweig, was doing graduate work at Yale. Even then, we communicated regularly by mail, writing long letters by hand. (Long distance phone calls were too expensive and typewriters too clumsy.)

After I married, the four of us traveled to be together, spending time in New York, New Haven, Palo Alto, San Francisco, Washington D.C. and of course Detroit, when the Rosenzweigs returned to visit their families. On those visits, Adelle and I spent as much time together as we could.

∾

The most important person I met in college was Bob Goren.

138

In the fall of my freshman year I was with Gloria, a friend from high school, in the lobby of the Wayne's Student Center. Suddenly, Gloria spotted a boy she knew and pulled me across the room.

"Come on, I want to introduce you to someone," she said.

He was eating an ice cream cone, and immediately offered us a taste. Gloria accepted but I shook my head. I was trying to figure out his age. He had a kind, open face and looked young. But he had very little hair on his head, which made me think he was much older than a teenager. Was he 25? 32? No, the face was too young. I was puzzled.

When I met Bob, I was still dating several other boys. I thought Bob was very nice, but wasn't especially interested at first. There was no instant physical attraction. Besides that, Bob was the social chairman of his local fraternity, Gamma Kappa Chi. I was quite disdainful, at 17, of fraternities and sororities, and stereotyped people who belonged to them as shallow.

One day between classes I stopped at the Student Center for a sandwich and discovered Bob at a table, reading. I sat down and we began to talk. He was studying for a class called "The Bible as Living Literature." He was majoring in Journalism and also taking a creative writing class. I realized immediately that this pleasant guy in his junior year had more depth than I had recognized. That was the first attraction.

A few days later he phoned me. He got my number from his friend and fraternity brother Mike, who got it from my best friend, Adelle. Mike wanted the four of us to double date and had urged Bob to call me. But when he did call, it was not to go out with Mike and Adelle. He invited me to go with him to a performance of *Romeo and Juliet* that was put on by Wayne's theater department. That scored more points in his favor.

That date was followed by a few more. I thought he was nice, but that was all. My lack of excitement was compounded by my mother's enthusiasm. "That Bob Goren is such a nice boy, such a gentleman."

"Oh, Mom," I protested, "he belongs to a *fraternity!*"

Our first kiss changed everything. We were riding in the back seat of his cousin Irving's car, with Irv's date in the passenger seat, on our way to a fraternity party. Bob had been playing his ukulele and singing. When I told him that he had a nice voice, he leaned over and kissed me. The kiss took us both by surprise, so we tried a few more, as a test: A-plus.

After that we went out more often, and I gradually lost interest in the other boys I'd been dating. Bob was 19 when we met, just two years older than I. In his senior year of high school he began to lose his hair. His mother took him to her beautician, a European woman who said she had a cream that would improve the situation. But it only made things worse. After learning that, I didn't care about his hair any more. I liked that he looked older. I always looked very young for my age (at every age) and his friends used to tease us: "Hey, Bob," they'd say, "are you out with your daughter again?"

By June, the end of my freshman year, I had no interest in dating anyone else. Bob was adamant, however, about not saying we were "going steady." He insisted that we had the right to date other people and didn't believe in labels or the bestowing of frat pins to prevent that from happening. But despite that, neither of us dated others after that first summer.

From the beginning, Bob was a tender and caring friend. There was a lot of turmoil within my family. My father had been released from Lafayette Clinic, the Detroit mental hospital where he had spent much of the past year, and was trying to adapt to a sales job he was ill suited for. He was still depressed, anxious and emotionally unavailable. My mother and I were at odds most of the time. More often than not, as soon as Bob and I were in his car I would tearfully pour out my most recent tale of woe. He held me, listened, commiserated, and gave me sensible advice. Then I would wipe my eyes and we would go to a movie or a party and have a good time. I found myself thinking about him more and more, spending time with him on campus between classes, talking on the phone every evening. This was not the same as the many crushes I'd had in high school, where the longing was only on my side, or situations when a boy liked me but I didn't return the feelings. This relationship was mutual, and by the middle of that first summer I realized I had really fallen in love.

By the end of summer, Bob and I knew we would be together for a long time, and he wanted his mother to meet me. He met my parents, of course, every time he picked me up for a date. He told me, later, that he had been worried about this meeting: What if she didn't like me? What if I didn't like her? In either case he would have felt very unhappy.

His mother was taking care of the children of his older sister, Helen, for a few days while Helen and her husband were on a short trip. We drove to Helen's house, and his mom was on the front porch while the toddlers, Henry and Kathy, played. The minute his mom and I met, there was instant rapport and acceptance. Bob needn't have worried for a minute! Later on, in the spring semester of my second year at Wayne, I met his father. He was equally welcoming and, on subsequent dinner visits to their home, he taught me how he made potato latkes or breaded veal chops.

I knew all the reasons I loved Bob, but I had trouble understanding why he loved me, when I felt depressed and withdrawn so much of the time and soaked the shoulder of his shirts with my tears at the start of every date. But I didn't question his love too strongly. As sad as I felt at home, I was equally happy with Bob, even just thinking about him. We got along well; we talked about everything, both personal and intellectual; there was a strong chemistry between us; we had fun together whatever we were doing, alone or with friends. Bob was open, had intellectual depth, good common sense, a strong sense of responsibility and the ability to love deeply.

One evening Bob, somewhat shyly, asked, "Would you consider marrying an old newspaper man?" Of course, I think he already knew the answer would be *yes*. I was near the end of my sophomore year and Bob was a senior. We decided to wait before becoming officially engaged, and then marry after he graduated. Later that year, however, working for the Detroit News, he saw the less glamorous side of newspaper work. The men were burned out, many of them alcoholic, and the job didn't pay very well. He decided instead to go to law school. There was another consideration in this decision: he probably would have been drafted into the army immediately after his graduation and he wanted to avoid that.

We agreed to become officially engaged on my next birthday, in 1953, when I would be 20. My birthday falls in April, but Bob couldn't wait to surprise me. On *his* birthday, in February, he presented me with a beautiful marquis-cut diamond engagement ring. We were at my parents' house, just before dinner. My mother was ecstatic and phoned Bob's parents to come over and celebrate that very evening. His parents, of course, were not surprised about the ring, since his mother had helped him pick it out. They loved me as much as my parents loved Bob, and we shared a joyous meal together that night.

We planned at first to marry after I graduated, in June of the following year. But Bob had enough money saved from his bar mitzvah and other family gifts for us to survive for 6 months and we moved the date to December of '53, marrying during our Christmas vacation. 1953 was a glorious year.

Adulthood

∽

Marriage: The Early Years
Jewish in Germany: Three Brief Stories
After France: Re-entry
Early Parenthood
Sharon
Marriage: Keeping it Together
Seeking a Spiritual Life: Religion, Poetry and Psychology
Humanistic and Spiritual: A Paradoxical Resolution

Judith and Bob in France, 1956

Marriage: The Early Years

༄

After Bob and I married, we lived for almost two years in a small apartment in Detroit, near Dexter and Broadstreet. We had a living room, bedroom, kitchen and bathroom and some inexpensive furniture we bought at a discount from Ruby's furniture store. During that time, Bob completed his last year and a half of law school; I completed the last half of my senior year at Wayne and was a long-term emergency substitute teacher for one semester at Cass Tech, where I had been a student only four years earlier. Between my salary and the money Bob had from his bar mitzvah, we lived well. When law school was over, Bob studied and took the bar exam.

Then he received his draft notice. He had been deferred from the military during undergrad and law school years and until the bar exam was over, but now had to serve in the army. Bob Goren, a gentle soul who liked to read, play the ukulele, write songs and sleep until noon on Sundays, was going to be a soldier. We joked that our country would be in good hands.

When Bob left for his two months of basic training at Fort Leonard Wood, Missouri, I was devastated. He was my main emotional support. During the day I taught journalism at Northeastern High School, in Detroit, where I had been hired when the Cass Tech job ended. I was responsible for the newspaper and the yearbook. After school, I visited one or both mothers in two different hospitals. Both our mothers had been diagnosed with cancer: Evelyn, age 48, had ovarian cancer, and Fanny, in her early 50's, had breast cancer. Both cases were serious and painful, and had metastasized before they were seen by doctors. In 1955 treatment was not sophisticated. At night, alone in our apartment, I cried.

As a private in the army, Bob scarcely had access to a working phone. Most of our communication was through handwritten letters, sent via U.S. mail, slowly. Just when I thought I wouldn't see him again for months, however, the army decided to give the new recruits a 10-day Christmas leave. Before I could wipe my eyes, he was home and once again he could sleep until noon. It was Christmas vacation for the schools, as well, so we spent every minute alone together when we were not visiting our mothers at their respective hospitals. This time when he left I was calmer, trusting that I would survive our separation and laughing at myself for having being so upset previously.

One day Bob sent word that he was on sick leave, very ill with a high fever. The soldiers were being taught how to deal with tropical diseases and listening to lectures about how to survive in jungles by crawling along the ground. However, it was February in Missouri, and they had been lying in the snow, getting soaking wet and freezing. Almost everyone came down with pneumonia.

Bob had previously applied for a weekend pass to meet me in St. Louis. I had my plane tickets and went because I knew he was ill. When I got to our hotel room, he was in bed with chills and a 104 degree fever. We phoned the hotel doctor, got some medication, and I did crossword puzzles at his bedside as he slept.

We had another sad farewell, thinking we wouldn't see one another for several more months, and then Bob had mixed news: when basic training was over, he would be sent to San Antonio, Texas. The bad news was that the army had no use for lawyers and he was to be trained as a dental assistant. The good news was that I could go with him to Texas and we could live together off-base.

Before we left for Texas, there was a long, sad delay. Bob's Uncle Harry had arranged for Bob to be placed on an extended leave because of the critical condition of his mother. It was not clear if she would survive much longer. Harry was also trying to pull official strings to get Bob assigned to a desk job in Detroit. He didn't ask Bob if he wanted that; he just went ahead and started the process. By that time, my mother had left the hospital and was managing at home.

Life at home was depressing, and we felt helpless. We were hoping for a respite, hoping to be forced to go to Texas. But we felt like bad children trying to say that to Harry. He was not to be thwarted, ever, and what good children would not want to be at their mothers' bedsides? We waited. No army job materialized in Detroit. Fanny, who was suffering greatly, passed away just before Bob was due in Texas. We stayed for the funeral and *shiva*, said goodbye to my family with feelings of sadness, guilt and anticipation, and then drove away to a new life.

∽

Once we had settled into our rented apartment with a pool, in San Antonio, I began to feel a pervasive, constant anxiety. Until then, my life had been busy every moment. I had a job, two mothers to tend, a sense of purpose. Now, very suddenly, I was displaced: no job, no time structure and as yet no friends. Bob was gone all day at his dental training. I tried to pretend I was just on a vacation, but I didn't feel that way. I needed a focus.

In the evenings I had a useful role to play: I had to quiz Bob on the names of teeth and dental instruments. His goal was to be one of the top three in his dental assistant class. The "prize" was the opportunity to choose any location in the United States where there was an army base to carry out the rest of his assignment. It's an interesting game: Where would you most like to be sent? He had in mind Washington, DC, Denver or San Francisco.

But now there was a new turn of events. All his striving for the prize had been for naught, even though he had, indeed, ranked first in his dentistry class. His entire unit was being shipped "overseas," which meant either to Korea or Europe. In this situation, he had no choice as to location. The war between North and South Korea was over, but the area still needed U.S. involvement to maintain the peace. If he went to Korea, I could not be with him. We both obsessed about Korea until finally good news arrived: Bob was to be sent to France. He had to travel with his unit, but I could join him later. Once again we said goodbye, but this time we felt more hopeful and excited about the months ahead. Bob left, and I returned to Detroit to break up our apartment, say goodbye to my family, and pack a trunk for France.

In 1956 there was little tourism in Europe. World War II had ended just over a decade earlier. Flights to France were way beyond our means. I booked passage on an ocean liner, the United States. I had paid for tourist class, but when I got on the boat that section was overcrowded, while there was an excess of first class rooms. I lucked out, sharing a pleasant room with a young woman from Holland. The ship was filled with school teachers traveling abroad for the first time so I didn't feel lonely. The voyage took four days. The first three days we hit the tail end of a hurricane, and the ship rocked terribly. Most of the passengers stayed in their cabins, sea-sick. I found that if I went out on the deck and actually watched the high waves, I felt less queasy than inside. I found it very exciting to hang on to the high railing and move up and down with the ocean swells. In the dining hall, there were times when all the dishes slid to one end of the table, then to the other, often spilling in someone's lap.

The ship finally docked at Le Havre. Bob and I, today, have differing memories of how I got to Paris: I thought he met me at the dock and we went together; he believes I took a train and he met me at the station. In any event, I got to Paris, we were reunited and it was heavenly. The only cloud, for Bob, was that he had not been assigned to the city of Paris. The young soldier in line ahead of Bob, a clueless kid just out of high school, was assigned Paris; Bob was assigned Verdun, the scene of terrible World War I battles, in the northeastern corner of France. Bob thought it was blatantly unfair that he had not been assigned Paris and he never quite got over it. However, he did find a good place for us to live. It was off the army base, in the center of Verdun, but he was very worried that I would not like it.

I, on the other hand, was thrilled simply to *be* in France. All the villages looked to me like they were movie sets for fairy tales. The houses were shaped like the kind children are taught to draw: a rectangle with a triangle for a roof. In front of each house was a mound: sometimes a bale of hay, sometimes a pile of manure to use as fertilizer. The roads were curvy, narrow, and dangerous. There was no center line, and the curves made it impossible to see oncoming traffic. Traffic was sparse, but the French drivers were notorious speeders, so as a driver approached a curve, he honked loudly as a warning. The villages were small and, where they ended, the sides of the roads were lined with trees. I expected to see Hansel and Gretel coming out of the forest, chased by an old witch. I was charmed by it all.

༄

For the first two weeks in Verdun, we stayed at a hotel, *le Coq Hardi*, until our rental space in a private home was vacated and ready for us. We were enchanted by the canopied bed, the dark maroon velvet comforter and drapes, the down pillows, and the wonderful croissants for breakfast each morning. (Croissants had not yet crossed the ocean to the U.S.)

In the mornings when Bob left for the army base, I explored the town on foot, locating the important sites such as a laundromat, *patisserie,* and places to buy groceries. In the evening we had wonderful French dinners *à l'hôtel*. The cost was about $1.75 a person for an entrée. After dinner, with no phone, movies or TV, we retired to our room, happy to be together at last.

Soon our new apartment was ready. It was a single room on the third floor of a 200 year old stone house, located on a hill, the highest point in Verdun, next door to the old stone cathedral where the bells chimed every hour. I thought it was incredibly romantic, like a room out of *La Boheme*, minus the consumption. There was only one problem with the set-up: the bed was only wide enough for one person. During the two weeks we waited, we didn't get much sleep. The owners could not provide us with a larger bed. We were waiting for a couple in the room on the floor below to leave so that we could move into their apartment. A single soldier would then rent our 3rd floor space.

The 2nd floor apartment was much more spacious: a very large room holding a double bed, an armoire for our clothing, a table and chairs for eating, a sofa and chair for reading in the evenings, and a small sink. Adjacent to that room was a long, narrow, closet-like space equipped with shelves for food, dishes and utensils, as well as a small stove and a bathtub that could be covered with a large board when we were preparing food. We joked about how it was possible to save time by taking a bath while stirring the spaghetti sauce on the stove.

We had been in this room less than a month when Bob got word that his father, Sam, was gravely ill from a heart attack and Bob was needed at home. In such cases, the army sends the soldier but not the spouse. Once again, we were to be separated. I decided to use that time to meet my mother's cousin, Carmen, and her young family, who lived just outside of Paris. Borrowing the telephone of our landlord, we called and made the necessary arrangements with her husband, Jean Baptendier, who fortunately was fluent in English. I went to Paris with Bob; he left for the airport and I met Jean, who drove me to their home.

During that visit I made use of my college French, since the rest of Jean's family did not speak English. Although Carmen and my mother had never met, our cousin was most warm and hospitable. Her children, at first a bit shy, soon were vying for whose turn it was to sit on my lap. It was the start of a life-long relationship, fulfilling the dream of my mother, who never did have an opportunity to travel to France. Although there were many years when we were out of contact, we resumed visits in later decades.

Bob's arrival at home lifted his father's spirits. He lived another two years, able to enjoy Gary, our first child, after our return. But Sam's heart was weak; he finally succumbed to another heart attack as he sat alone in his bedroom at Bob's sister's house on a summer morning in 1959. He was the third of our parents to leave us in three years.

Before I arrived in France, Bob had ordered a car for us, an Italian Fiat Spyder convertible five-gear red two-seater sports car. Shortly after he returned from the trip to see his father, the car was ready for us at an auto dealership in Paris. We went by train, stayed overnight, and the next morning picked up our car. We were as excited as kids on Christmas/Hanukkah morning. The car dealer was near the Champs- Elysees. We took the Fiat for a test drive and felt like we were driving in an eggshell. Fortunately, traffic in 1956 in Paris was not the way it is today, or we wouldn't have lasted two seconds. Everyone, driving or walking, stopped to see our red Fiat. They had never seen anything like it. We had never been the center of so much attention as we were while driving in that traffic circle near the Etoille.

We loved that first drive back from Paris to Verdun, all four hours. What a wondrous new toy we had! And it only cost $2,500.

❧

Soon after we returned with our new Fiat, a notice appeared in an army newsletter that a 2nd grade teacher was urgently needed at the American Elementary School at Etain Air Force Base, about twenty miles from Verdun. Although I had taught high school, I had no training in elementary education. I wasn't even sure if I wanted a job like that. But I decided to apply. If nothing else, it was a good excuse to take out the Fiat by myself. On a beautiful September morning I removed the convertible top (it wasn't automatic; it had to be unclipped and shoved by hand into its storage spot in the back of the car) and drove out through the French countryside for the interview.

The principal begged me to come on board and offered me all the help I needed. Even though I protested ("I don't know anything about teaching second grade," I told him) he still insisted. The present class had 44 children, two of whom were emotionally disturbed and disruptive. The teacher was highly experienced and dedicated, but she needed help.

"We'll split the class fairly" he promised, "and she'll mentor you."

In the end, I took the job, and loved it because I loved the children. I have a photo somewhere of the 22 children who were in my classroom. I can remember the first names of almost every one of them, how they behaved and how well they could read. In my heart they are still seven years old.

Having taken care of a place to live, a car to get around, and a job to fill my time and give us added spending money, our thoughts turned to travel. Europe was ours to explore. The rest of the year truly became an extended honeymoon (even though we had already been married for two years). We visited all the World War I battle sites in and around Verdun. We were four hours drive from Paris, where we spent many weekends, and two hours from Luxembourg, where we often went to change dollars into French francs at a better rate than we could get in France. We drove to Brussels and Holland, and visited army buddies in Germany. We sang duets in the car, holding hands while watching out for the crazy drivers behind us who honked to pass, or heading toward us around those blind curves. We drove to nearby cities: Rouen, Nancy, Strasbourg. Wherever we went, we were almost the only tourists. Arthur Frommer's guidebook, *France on $5.00 a Day,* was brand new, an invaluable resource. Frommer in hand, we explored and ate our way through every village, town and city in our path like two kids discovering a world of magic.

We had unexpected adventures, and survived: at Thanksgiving, we drove to London with new army friends, Joe and Hope Blonsky, taking a car ferry across the English Channel. On our return at night, Joe's car had a flat tire on a narrow, icy road, and Joe and Bob had to change it in the snow without a flashlight. During a Christmas leave, we took a train to the French Riviera, where Bob lost his wallet with money and army ID cards. After an hour of panic, we retrieved everything at the local bakery which had been our first stop, and marveled at the kindness and honesty of the people who had held it for us, awaiting our return. When spring arrived we toured Switzerland. On the day we had to go home we left too close to sunset and drove back to Verdun in the dark on a treacherous road through the French Alps, arriving at 2:00 a.m. trembling from the tension of the night drive.

In June, when school was over, we took a long trip to Italy, visiting Venice, Florence and Rome. At the Vatican, we joined a throng of thousands who were gathered in St. Peter's square to see the Pope. I was three months pregnant, and very happy about it, although I didn't look or feel pregnant and could scarcely believe the good news. What if the doctor had been mistaken? As if in answer to my question, as the Pope on his balcony blessed the crowd below, I had my first and only experience of nausea, throwing up into a little rain hat I wore and then, hoping no one had seen me, finding a trash can to dispose of the hat and its contents. After that I never questioned the doctor's judgment.

Italy turned out to be our last trip before the army sent me home. I had to travel back to the United States by the 6th month of my pregnancy to qualify for a free flight. My mother was now quite ill again; it was definitely time for me to return. Bob's two years of service would not end until December.

In August, our long honeymoon, which had begun with a separation, now ended with one, as I tearfully packed my steamer trunk, left Bob alone in our room, and flew back to Detroit, courtesy of the United States Army.

Being Jewish in Germany: Three Brief Stories

∞

1956: Visiting Dachau

On a fall weekend, we visited an army buddy, Jerry, whom we had met and spent time with during Bob's dental training days in San Antonio. Jerry and his wife were now in Munich. We spent a pleasant time with them, catching up on events that occurred after all of us had left Texas.

Munich was close to the former concentration camp at Dachau. Since we were driving, we decided to take a sight-seeing detour on our return trip. It was a beautiful spring day as we drove down a country road toward Dachau in our red Fiat Spyder convertible, with the top open to the sky and breeze.

In 1956, the existence of the camps and their purpose was known to the world, but it would be several years before the plethora of written accounts and film footage, both documentary and fictional, depicted the holocaust for public awareness. Because I knew little and had not given much conscious thought to our destination, it surprised me to find that as far as twenty miles from Dachau, my body tensed, my breathing became shallow and my sense of dread increased. It was as if the horrors that had happened a little more than a decade earlier still permeated the air we were breathing.

When we arrived at the camp, which now was open for public viewing, a strong resistance gripped my soul.

"You go," I urged Bob. "I'll wait for you in the car."

"Come with me," he said. "You won't feel any better sitting here." He was right. I didn't want to see what was ahead, but neither did I want to be alone with whatever lingered in the atmosphere.

We walked quickly through the camp, across packed earth where no grass grew, slowing only to read the signs that explained the use of the various rooms and chambers: this room was where the people stripped, the next was where the "showers" released poisoned gas; another was the crematorium. Here were the chimneys where noxious smoke had filled the air in the very space where we now were standing. It felt almost surreal that, on this silent weekday morning at Dachau, we were the only people viewing the site of such atrocities. I felt shaky, weak and queasy, overwhelmed by the realization that, had I been born in Germany, I would have been killed in childhood. The thought went through me like an electric prod and instantly strengthened my weak, if negative, Jewish identification.

1957: Fasching Week

The following spring we revisited Munich during Fasching week, a time of high festivity and a carnival-like atmosphere, similar to Mardi Gras. I was not eager to take the trip, but Bob viewed it as a cultural event and wanted to witness it. We went into a *bierstube* for a drink. Everyone was costumed, singing and pounding their mugs on wooden tables, just like in a happy movie. I could not get into the fun. I watched everyone, wondering: *Would they hate me if they knew I was Jewish? Would they have turned me in 12 years ago?* As for the younger ones, I wondered what anti-Semitic ideas they had learned from their parents. My discomfort felt close to paranoia. The contrast was remarkable: with the entire country in celebration, Bob was excited to see the show, and I, close to tears, was an outsider who wanted to leave, to return to our cozy room in Verdun, where I felt safe.

1980 and '82: Two workshops in Heidelberg

Over two decades later, I had more opportunities to explore my feelings about Jewishness in a German setting. An American friend and psycho-therapy colleague, Arlene, had recently married and moved to Heidelberg, where her American husband had settled after his army stint in the '50's. Lonely for her American friends, she invited many of us to Germany to present workshops and seminars on new ideas and techniques to enhance personal growth. In 1980, Arlene invited me to present a journal writing workshop to a small group of her colleagues and clients. The idea intrigued me, and I accepted the invitation. We met in an intimate environment in

Arlene's living room. I found the group to be warm and interested in my presentation and in the writing exercises. Uncomfortable about being the only Jew in this group, I very consciously avoided any reference to the subject of Jewishness, and the issue never arose.

Two years later, I wrote a letter to Arlene about a Jewish woman I had recently met, Julia Press, who conducted personal growth workshops based on universal spiritual principles. Intrigued, Arlene invited Julia to lead a weekend on spirituality for a group in Heidelberg. Julia asked me to accompany her. I went, in part, to deepen my new friendship with Julia, as well as to maintain contact with Arlene.

When we arrived in Heidelberg, my old feeling of uneasiness about being Jewish in Germany was even more pronounced. Initially, the group seemed large and impersonal: there were over 40 people, only some of whom spoke English, and we met in a rented space that lacked the warmth of Arlene's home. The group knew from a conversation at the start of the first day that both Julia and I were Jewish.

My previous workshop had been quite structured. Julia, however, leads groups in a free-flowing manner. Whatever is moving deeply in someone's heart and soul is invited to be presented and the work proceeds from there. Anything may arise.

Midway into the first day, a woman burst out at me, "I wish you hadn't come!" I was stunned. Later, sobbing, she explained her emotion to the group. Her father had been a Nazi storm trooper. My presence as a Jew, along with Julia, doubled her deep sense of shame and guilt.

"I'm sorry," she said. "I just want to get rid of this pain! It's not about Judith."

Her confession opened up discussion among the entire group. The collective guilt they carried on behalf of their parents' generation poured forward. It was a revelation to me that Germans of my generation felt this way. As the stories continued, all of us wept together.

I have continued to correspond by e-mail with several friends in Germany. Most were children, as I was, during World War II; some were not even born. Yet they feel accountable for the actions of their families and their country. I still do not know how to forgive the perpetrators of the Holocaust and perhaps I never will. At the same time, I care deeply for my German friends. Anna, the woman whose outburst was so hurtful, brought me a symbolic gift two years later, when she joined me in another circle with Julia in Boston. It is a piece of wood from a tree that once grew in her yard. It is shaped like a perfect heart. I keep it on a special shelf.

After France: Re-entry

∾

When I arrived back in Michigan in August of 1957, I stayed at the home of Bob's sister Helen, in Huntington Woods, a suburb two miles north of Detroit. She and her husband, Harold, had three young children and the atmosphere was lively. My parents and my brother Dick were still living in the house on Appoline. My father was depressed again, although managing to minimally care for my mother. I could barely tolerate the aura of accumulated tension and sorrow when I entered that house and felt I could be more useful if I lived elsewhere and visited daily. My mother was weak from the progression of her ovarian cancer and the surgeries she had undergone. She had already lived far beyond the prognosis of her doctors, almost willing herself to stay alive until I returned from Europe and until she could see her first grandchild.

Bob was not due to be released from the army until December, 1957. However, a compassionate friend of my parents intervened without our knowledge. He was a surgeon who had been a Captain during WWII. He knew how the army worked and he knew our situation. He wrote a letter on Bob's behalf requesting an emergency leave for him to take care of ill family. In November, Bob was sent home from France. Once he arrived, the army released him early.

We needed to find a home of our own before our baby was born and had planned to look at houses in Detroit. However, everyone we knew urged us to move to Oak Park, a new and fast-growing suburb situated between Detroit and Huntington Woods. Houses were affordable and many young Jewish couples lived there. We purchased our first home, a small 3-bedroom ranch, a few weeks before I gave birth to Gary. He was the first baby born in Oak Park on New Years Day in 1958, which started him out in life with notoriety in the local newspaper.

My mother was thrilled beyond words to be with her grandson, although, after his first few months, she no longer had the strength to hold him. She spent many weeks that year in Harper Hospital. It was against the rules to bring babies inside to visit, so Bob would drive to Detroit and perch Gary on his shoulders outside her third floor window, where she could look out and see them. Eventually, she was too weak to get out of bed to do even that. In April of 1959, three months after Gary's first birthday and four years after her initial diagnosis, she died.

Watching my mother suffer those last months in the hospital was unbearable. She, who had long complained about her weight at 140 lbs., was down to about 80. She was hooked up to IVs and couldn't turn over without help. She was weak, in pain, and could barely speak or even respond to stories about Gary. I had no knowledge and no guidance about how to be with someone at the end stage of life. I coped with the situation in the only way I knew: I shortened my visits and deadened my feelings.

The day she died, I came home from the hospital with Bob, my father and his cousin, a rabbi from New York. I went directly into my bedroom, lay down on the bed and finally started to let my tears flow, when my father knocked on the door.

"Please come out and make us some tea," he said. "Don't cry now. I haven't cried yet, myself."

I went into the kitchen and made tea. My deep grief went underground again, turning into a chronic low-level depression that didn't abate for several years, when the dam finally broke in therapy sessions and the suppressed pain and loss of the past several years flooded out.

Early Parenthood

❦

Shortly after Gary's second birthday, Steve was born. As infants, the boys resembled one another, with big blue eyes and bald heads which then grew fine, pale blond hair. Both were large babies. When I learned I was pregnant once more, I strongly hoped for a girl, although I was convinced that I would have a boy who resembled the other two. Only eighteen months after Steve was born, Nancy arrived, tiny, with a full head of dark hair. On the delivery table, I laughed and cried with delight.

Giving birth to two sons and a daughter, all within less than four years, was both the most loving, bonding, exhilarating time in our lives, and the most stressful. At night when the little ones were asleep, Bob and I would tiptoe into their bedrooms to gaze at them and feel the joy and awe of being the parents of three beautiful sleeping children.

"Sleeping" is the key word here: during waking hours, life was much more complex. It was a new world for which we had no training. I was home all day with the children: one balking against going to nursery school, one being toilet trained, one in diapers and on bottles. My salvation came in help from Bob's sister Helen and my new step-mom and mentor, Sharon, whom my father had married just days before I gave birth to Steve. I was also fortunate to be able to socialize with friendly young neighbors with small children and to have excellent household help, our beloved Josie Keys, who did cleaning and laundry for our family for many years.

Bob landed a demanding job with a good law firm and traveled downtown every morning to work, driving back home in evening rush-hour traffic. Every day I waited impatiently for the hour when Bob would return home to help with the children and I could have an adult conversation. Every day Bob dreamed of returning home to kiss his family and take a nap. Our conflicting expectations were a source of new disharmony between us.

I loved my husband, my children and my home; yet there was a rising tide of sadness inside of me. I had never resolved any of my family conflicts from late adolescence. A few months before my mother died I had suffered an early miscarriage, which put me into a depression, even though I was not yet ready for a second pregnancy or baby. Bob was advised to take me to Florida for a week to get over it, but the separation from Gary made me even sadder. My mother's last year of life was Gary's first, and I had postponed grieving as I focused on motherhood. Bob was dealing with new stress at work, but didn't talk about it. We had never learned how to address conflict, and dealt with it by pretending things were fine.

Meanwhile, the children grew and thrived. I hated when they fought or pushed or cried. I loved dressing them, kissing them, feeding them, bathing them, putting them in clean pajamas and rocking them to sleep. I loved being with them as they began to walk, to talk, to ask questions. It was a time of loving and a time of angst.

As the children reached nursery school age, I began to yearn for something in addition to motherhood. This was in the early 1960's, when Betty Friedan's classic analysis, *The Feminine Mystique*, was still being written. I was living what she called "the problem with no name." Even after the book came out, I was too preoccupied to read it for a number of years.

Sharon

◦◦

About a year after my mother died, Sharon, a long-time friend of my father's youngest sister, moved from Chicago to Detroit and phoned my father. They made a date to meet for lunch. The day after they met, my father phoned and invited me to lunch. When we talked, I noticed how he was glowing; he looked ten years younger and incredibly happy.

"I met a woman," he said. "I really like her. She's feminine and attractive, and she thinks like a man." In those pre-feminist days (1960) I heard that as the compliment he intended it to be. I was very happy to see him looking so well after such a long time. Sharon was 48, nine years younger than my father.

"I want you to meet her," he said. I agreed. I liked her, too: she was warm and straightforward, attractive and stylishly dressed, intelligent and a good listener. Sharon had moved because both of her married daughters lived in the Detroit suburbs. As they had children, she wanted to be physically close to their families. Her first husband had died at home (unexpectedly, of a heart attack) when the girls were in their teens, and she had continued to work as a medical transcriptionist and to raise them alone.

Only three weeks after they met, my father and Sharon married. The date was April 3. I was pregnant with my second child, but my father didn't want to wait until after the baby was born. In fact, he joked that he was pre-empting my birthday, April 5, by choosing that date. (There was still some of the young boy in him, anxious lest his younger siblings "get there first.") They had a private ceremony with a judge. A week later, I was in the hospital, in labor, and Sharon was right there with me. Steven was born on April 9.

On Passover, eight days later, my father's new bride was standing in my Oak Park kitchen making *matzah brei* for our many aunts and uncles at Steve's *bris* (ritual circumcision). I was forever grateful to Sharon for taking over a social task I didn't even know had to be performed. We held the *bris* not because it had special meaning for either Bob or me, but because Steven was to receive his Jewish name, *Schmuel,* in memory of Bob's father, Sam. The ceremony was important to Sam's brothers and to Bob's sister. As the Goren and Wise relatives milled around in the living room, I hid in the bedroom until the worst was over.

Sharon had experience as a teenager caring for her many nieces and nephews, and later for her own daughters and their children. She became my "Dr. Spock" for child rearing advice. When Stevie was colicky and cried, she laid him over her forearm, tummy down, and gently patted his back. The pressure on the stomach seemed to ease the pain of the colic. When Gary, who was almost 2 ½ when his brother entered the world, had one of his mini-tantrums, Sharon knew just how to distract him. Gary was late acquiring speech and called her Nini; the name has stayed in our family through the next two generations.

Sharon had grown up in a large family, with friends and relatives always in and out of one another's apartments. My father, too, had lived near a large extended family in Detroit, but he found all the visiting chaotic and didn't enjoy it. (When I was growing up, I scarcely knew who these aunts, uncles and cousins were, although they lived within walking distance from us.) Sharon wanted her daughters and our family to visit them freely with all the babies and toddlers. My father vetoed this plan.

"We'll visit the children in their homes," he said. "One family at a time."

That began the tradition of Sunday visits from the grandparents, and possibly the beginning of a depression that Sharon carried for many years. She was feisty and outspoken, but my father was a Man-to-be-Obeyed. After a while she gave up arguing over the issue, but her anger did not leave her; it only went silent. Although she went daily to her job at a local hospital, for some years it was evident that she was depressed.

Then, too, there were Herman's mood swings: before they married, he had not told her, and no one else had warned her, that he recently had been hospitalized with severe depression and that his effusive verbalizations were the other side of the spectrum. When she found that her feisty anger only made things worse between them, she clammed up. Their mutual and sometimes coinciding times of depression began early and lasted throughout their marriage. Sharon brightened up only around the grandchildren.

Sharon always expressed wonder and appreciation at the way she had been accepted by Dick and me into our family. This puzzled me. I liked her and was very happy for my father. Evidently, Sharon knew several families where the second wife was not so well accepted by the adult children. She had been nervous about being in that situation and was relieved and grateful to find she was fully accepted by us. She treated our family as she did her own, not distinguishing between "his" and "hers" when it came to love.

She introduced me to people as her daughter, and considered my children as much her grandkids as she did the children of her own two daughters. However, I never felt comfortable introducing her as my mom, or calling her "mother." A person can have many daughters, but there is only one mother. I would have felt disloyal to mine, even though she was gone, had I done differently. Fortunately, Sharon understood and it was not a problem.

Herman and Sharon had been married 18 years when my father had a stroke that sent him to the hospital. He was there three days, in a coma, and then he was gone, at the age of 73. During those three days I sat with him and talked to him. He held my hand, squeezing it to let me know he heard me, but he was unable to speak. As unhappy as I was, his way of leaving seemed less cruel to me than the suffering my mother had endured over her last several years.

After my father died, Sharon and I grieved together. Her frozen feelings melted; her sobbing brought her back to life. After true grieving, her light but long-standing depression lifted. She became once again the vibrant woman she had been when she met my father. Our relationship deepened as we spent more time together over the next 20-some years. Our loving friendship greatly enriched my life.

Marriage: Keeping it Together

෪

...let there be spaces in your togetherness
and let the winds of heaven dance between you.

From ***The Prophet***, *by Kahil Gibran*

The conflicts and dissention Bob and I felt as work and parenthood changed our lives came and went over the following years as new situations arose, but they did not erode the solid, loving aspects of our relationship. Marriage is a dynamic, not a static entity, and we rode the waves as they crested and fell. As our outer world shifted with growing children and new work activities, so did our "contract" with each other. Our wishes and expectations had to be continually redefined and renegotiated. Looking backward from my present day perspective, I view our long-term marriage (57 years and still counting) as a series of phases:

During the first four years, we shared the concerns of having ill parents and interference by the U.S. Army. We didn't think of ourselves as "husband and wife," but as Bob and Judy, two people in love, with Europe as our playground for the year before we became parents.

The next phase, having a family and establishing Bob's law career, was distinctly different. Our needs conflicted, our expectations of one another were often unrealistic, and painful feelings were inevitable. It helped that we married in an era when couples were expected to stay together.

The third phase began when our children were about 8, 10 and 12. Bob and I hit a low point in our relationship. Our interests beyond the family were widely divergent. Bob was running his own law firm, trying cases all over the state of Michigan, and working very long hours. He wanted to get away, to travel and play tennis. I wanted *not* to travel, to stay home and explore the new world I was discovering of therapy and encounter groups and to write poetry. We looked at each other as if we were two strangers. We decided to stay together, to follow our own paths and see where that led. It was a scary decision, but not as scary as the thought of divorce. Beneath all the differences, we still felt love. And we both wanted stability for the children.

Gradually, as we became more of our own selves, we discovered a new respect for each other. Following our separate life passions had strengthened both of us. We noticed, once again, that we were living with interesting partners. We even began to sample one another's worlds. Bob was very supportive of my writing and came to all my poetry readings. He even came to a few weekend groups, just to see what they were all about. I took a few tennis lessons and agreed to travel with him.

By the time our children were in high school, we established a new kind of contract. I was working several evenings as a group therapist; Bob had a demanding career as organizer of a new law firm. We had ongoing negotiations about who would be home, who would fix dinner, who would go to events at the high school or help the kids with projects and when we would spend time alone together. We scheduled the "alone- time" carefully, not leaving it to chance. This was of crucial importance in maintaining closeness and intimacy.

At another level, we both had to learn how to express dissatisfaction without yelling, crying, withdrawing, denying, or making global accusations ("You **always**..." or "You **never**..."). This was a long learning process. Neither of us had learned, growing up, how to express our anger. I was taught not to feel mine; Bob was expected to be "nice." My anger exploded in tears and angry accusations; Bob used "I'm only trying to be nice" as a categorical defense, which simply inflamed me more. It took us years, perhaps decades, to learn how to communicate effectively when both of us were upset. We were helped and guided by our individual psychotherapy sessions, by my training and work as a therapist (if I remembered not to sound like a know-it-all), and by a large portion of love and common sense.

A new phase began when all three children were living apart from us at college. We had a quieter life at home with just two of us, and could synchronize our travels with the weeks the children were elsewhere, without disrupting their lives by being gone. Having learned more about how to communicate effectively, a new and more mature closeness and love grew between us. We were each busy and fulfilled with careers and separate out-side activities; this gave us renewed vigor to bring to our relationship when we were together. Each day we cleared our plans with one another and set a time to be together in the evening, to have a cup of tea and review what we had been doing.

Another chapter of our marriage began when the first grandchild was born and has continued to be a source of shared joy as eight other grand-children followed. By then our work hours were shorter and we scheduled much of our time around visits from the three young families, or trips to their homes. One family lived five minutes away; the other two locations were five hour drives, in different directions. Our visits with everyone were and continue to be a central part of our lives and an expansion of the love we share with our children and their children, as well as with each other.

Seeking a Spiritual Life:
Religion, Poetry and Psychology

∽

The Roots of Humanistic Judaism

In the early '60's, when our three children were still very young, I was determined that they not feel like outsiders in a Jewish world, as I had. I wanted to join a Reform Temple and send our children to Sunday school. I was too far removed from the Orthodox or Conservative beliefs and rituals to feel comfortable there, but would have considered joining one of the two major Reform congregations, although I did not feel a great affinity with either. I also wanted to understand and form a relationship with God, whatever that meant. Beyond educating my children, I felt a strong sense of personal quest.

Bob, however, wanted no part of organized religion. He grew up surrounded by a large, first generation family of adults and young cousins and felt secure about the cultural aspects of being Jewish. He had an Orthodox bar mitzvah, which he considered meaningless, and now was much like my father in his non-belief system.

We would have been hopelessly deadlocked, except for the advent of a new Reform congregation with a brilliant, charismatic young rabbi. Although Bob came reluctantly to our first service at the Birmingham Temple, he was intellectually hooked once he heard Rabbi Sherwin Wine speak. He agreed to join, along with many of our closest friends.

Early on, Rabbi Wine engaged the Temple members and the larger Jewish community in discussions of "What do we mean by the word God?" I was excited that at last someone was publicly addressing this enormous question that I had puzzled over internally for many years. There were both public forums and meetings within the Temple to discuss what we believed, which established rituals reflected our beliefs and which did not. Rabbi Wine opened up new pathways in our thinking. But the result was not what I had expected.

It's now history that the Birmingham Temple evolved from Reform to Humanistic Judaism, and still later, to Secular Humanistic Judaism. What began in 1963 as discussions in members' living rooms has now turned into an accepted world-wide movement of some 40,000 people. About a quarter of that number live in North America; the others reside in Israel, Europe and South America.

The emphasis in Secular Humanistic Judaism (SHJ) is on our Jewish heritage, culture, history, holidays, life cycle events and ethical behavior. There is a belief in human responsibility, both individually and collectively, as opposed to praying to a Supreme Being to intercede.

After many public and private discussions about God, Rabbi Wine finally said, "The word "God" has so many meanings for so many people that it has become meaningless." This happened during the first year of the Birmingham Temple, when we were still in transition. The word "humanistic" had just been introduced to our small congregation. To make a strong differentiation between humanism and more traditional beliefs, all references to the word "God" were dropped from our liturgy. Religious or "god-language" (spiritual, divine, sacred, mystery, holy, soul, mysticism) was dismissed as irrelevant. Looking back, I see this was essential in making a clear distinction between Reform and Humanistic Judaism. For Bob, this publicly expressed viewpoint was refreshing and in line with his own long-held beliefs. But for me it was a deep disappointment, prematurely ending the discussion which first drew me in and which, for me, was still incomplete.

The changes were highly controversial. Our congregation was on the front lines of Jewish community hostility during the months of debate in the '60's as the transition from Reform to Humanistic occurred. Once again I was in a familiar but uncomfortable place, at the edge of the greater Detroit Jewish community, most of whom considered us blasphemous for dropping God and continued to shun our congregation for many years.

Still, there were compelling reasons to stay. I had been deeply engaged by my intense participation in the early philosophical debates about God. Despite our differing philosophical points of view, both my husband and

I respected, admired and enjoyed listening to Rabbi Wine; his brilliance awed us. We felt a sense of social connection within the congregation. Most important, Bob would not have accepted any other congregation as an alternative; he firmly believed that Rabbi Wine was presenting us with a new Jewish movement, one that would be influential not only now but into the future. After months of inner conflict, I stayed even though God had to leave.

Our children, I suspect, would have stories similar to mine about feeling on the edge of a Jewish identification. They were in Sunday school during the years when the Temple was under open siege from the greater Detroit Jewish community and came in for their share of ostracism from other children, as I once did. *You're not really Jewish if you belong to the Birmingham Temple*, neighbors' children informed my young sons when they were waiting in the snow for the school bus one morning. *Your Rabbi doesn't even believe in God!*

As the first decade of the Birmingham Temple continued, our congregation began to be accepted and integrated into the larger Jewish community. The ostracism faded away and was replaced, in many cases, by respect for Rabbi Wine's rational-intellectual stance and personal integrity. On the positive side, I took an increasingly active role in our congregation. Mentored by Rabbi Wine, I revised an adult secular history of the Jews into 5th grade language, to be used as a Sunday school text. I was asked to serve as an associate editor for a new magazine, *Humanistic Judaism*, which would be distributed nationally. I was invited more than once to give readings of my poetry in lieu of a traditional Shabbat service. Many of our closest friends were part of the congregation, providing a pleasant social situation. My relationship to my own Judaism became more positive as our children grew; I enjoyed introducing them to family celebrations of the Jewish holidays, usually shared with Bob's sister's family.

Yet, once again, I found myself on the outer edge of a Jewish community, this time within my own congregation. While I was now connected to the Birmingham Temple socially and intellectually, and to Judaism historically and ethically, I was still marooned spiritually. Efforts to talk about this dilemma with my secular humanist friends led nowhere. "What do you mean by spiritual?" they asked me.

Because of the ban on "god-language," I had not even the vocabulary to make sense of my feelings. I discussed this dilemma at length, on more than one occasion, with Rabbi Wine. He was a caring and compassionate listener and he fully understood me. But he was not about to change his position.

"What we need," he said, "is a new vocabulary. We need someone creative, good with words, to find new ways to describe personal experience." I took his challenge to heart, but was not able to meet it. I had no new vocabulary to offer, only my longing, painful and wordless. Four decades later, in Sam Harris's *The End of Faith*, I found he, too, could find no other word for "spirituality" or "mysticism," and apologetically used both words in his writings. I felt validated.

Leaving for another temple was a non-solution. I had given up literal belief in the traditional God of the Torah, whom I believed to be an anthropomorphic representation of some Greater Reality (also banned language). I had long thought of the word "God" as pointing toward something infinitely larger than the historic character in the Old Testament. I could not accept the language of the Conservative or even the Reform prayer books, which spoke to God as an actual person, a literal figure to be feared, worshipped and praised. Yet I sensed that in abandoning all "god-language," our movement had blocked understanding of something significant, something for which I yearned and could not name.

Exploring Poetry and Psychology

For the first two decades that I belonged to the Birmingham Temple, I was also on a path of intense personal exploration. Just a year or two after the temple formed, I discovered that I had a passion for writing poetry. I took time for this pursuit in the afternoon when the children were napping or in nursery school. At first I wasn't sure that what I was writing was really poetry, but I signed up for classes and workshops and applied my learning to my work. The act of creating each new poem was a source of exhilaration.

A few years later, I explored every kind of group situation that passed through the greater Detroit area. These groups were loosely part of what the magazines of the day had labeled "the Human Potential Movement," or less empathically, the "touchy-feely" groups. As opportunities arose to experience this new world moving east from California, I was drawn, as if by a magnet, to participate in sensitivity and encounter groups, Transactional Analysis (TA) training, and, later, groups designed to expand conscious awareness. Although many of my acquaintances questioned or teased me, I was fascinated and unapologetic. I learned from my very first experience that I had an intuitive grasp of group dynamics and knew that this was a field in which I wanted to seek training as a leader. Looking back, the events of that era feel to me like a calling, although at the time I didn't use that word. I was simply stepping from one growth opportunity to the next: each new workshop or training session made me feel excited and alive.

My experiences in groups often stirred up unresolved feelings from my younger years, which led me into individual psychotherapy. I participated in a very intense form of psychological work popular at that time, Bioenergetic Therapy. This was based on the teaching of Alexander Lowen, M.D., a psychiatrist whose books I devoured. Bioenergetics worked with the body as well as the mind, with a series of exercises designed to allow the muscles to release repressed emotions. I experienced depths of grief and rage I never knew existed, let alone in me! It was difficult emotional work, but over time it freed up energy for a deeper enjoyment of my life.

Eventually my two paths led to conducting local writing workshops and to many publications of my poetry, as well as to leading personal growth and TA groups. By the late '70's I had a large number of clients. Because state licensing laws had become stricter, I needed more credentials to legally continue my chosen career as a psychotherapist. I enrolled in a doctoral program and earned my Ph.D. in Humanistic and Clinical Psychology in 1983, just in time to celebrate that event along with my 50th birthday. *

*A more detailed account of my career can be found in "Sharing the Journey: A Psychotherapist Reflects on her Work," available on the web at Amazon.com or i.Universe.com

Being Humanistic and Spiritual:
A Paradoxical Resolution

∽

By the 1980's, I was drawn to explore spirituality and transformation of consciousness. I attended workshops, seminars and retreats, read voraciously, meditated regularly, and sought out various spiritual teachers and friends on similar paths. I attended several retreats in California with an American spiritual teacher, Richard Moss. Through this work I had met Julia Press, with whom I traveled to Germany in 1982.

It was through my work with Julia that I found the "missing piece" that had eluded me in my affiliation with Humanistic Judaism.

In her everyday life, Julia is a wife, mother and grandmother, living in the grounded reality of the material world. Simultaneously, she is always connected to the world of mystical consciousness. Her expanded awareness is fully integrated into her daily actions and informs her relationships. Although she is not a Buddhist, among many of us who know her well there is agreement that she has the qualities of a Bodhisattva (the Buddhist term for one who has attained enlightenment and, through wisdom and compassion, helps others move toward that goal.) She has a rich understanding, both experiential and intellectual, of Kabbalah, or mystical Judaism.

One of the most loving and compassionate beings I have ever had the good fortune to know, she was to become, and has remained, the pivotal mentor of my transformational process, as well as an intimate and beloved personal friend.

Our Spiritual Community

The opportunity to travel with Julia in 1982 deepened a burgeoning friendship, which has continued over the decades. Since first meeting Julia, I

175

have been part of a loosely woven spiritual community of about 80 people. We have no name and Julia has no title; we refer to ourselves as a "family of friends." The men and women who are part of this circle live in many places, scattered over the U.S. and Canada, Germany and Argentina. We are Jewish, Protestant, Catholic, Buddhist and secular. There are among us doctors and writers, artists and massage therapists, attorneys and teachers, psychotherapists and professors, students and grandmothers. We are a non-residential community, except for a week every summer when forty or fifty of us gather at a retreat center near Toronto.

We meet with no pre-determined agenda, sitting in a circle in a large meeting room. We begin in silence, and whatever deeply arises in someone is brought forward to the group. We have learned to listen to one another without trying to give advice or "fix" anything. The experience of being listened to with full attention has a healing quality of its own. When the speaker feels complete, he or she conveys that to the group. After a few moments, someone else steps forward. Sometimes energies arise spontaneously, and we sing, or chant, or dance, or join hands and sit in deep silence. In the unscheduled afternoons, we may walk, meet in small groups, have one-on-one conversations, write, swim, nap or read in the sun. Then we join one another again in the meeting room.

During the year, we all stay in touch through phone and group e-mails. Those who live close enough to one another meet locally throughout the year to meditate, study and explore our spiritual process. We read or watch videos and informally discuss the work of other spiritual teachers, such as Eckhardt Tolle, Deepak Chopra, A.H. Almaas, Adyshanti, Richard Moss, Ken Wilbur, Pema Chodron and Jack Kornfield. The goal of our work is to live with full consciousness and compassion, integrating our spiritual knowledge into our relationships with others. For all of us, this is the work of a lifetime.

A Humanistic Mystic?

For many years I experienced two parts of my inner self in continual debate. One part was totally rational, like Sherwin Wine; the other part was open to Mystery, like Julia Press. Whenever I heard about, read, or experienced something that was not easily explainable in rational terms, the inner debate began. Neither side ever won or lost, and my inner conflict continued. I often fantasized that the two real people with those names, both of intense importance in my life, would meet, talk and reach agreement, so I could stop my inner arguments. Sometimes I pictured Sherwin and Julia having a quiet conversation in Sherwin's office. I would be in the room, listening quietly, or perhaps asking questions. At other times, I envisioned them on a stage before a large audience, in a profound discussion about the nature of life, death, religion and spiritual issues.

This never happened, for a number of reasons, the chief ones being distance, lack of time and probable disinterest: Julia lives in New England and when she does visit Michigan, every moment of her time is committed, as was Sherwin Wine's; and the issue of reconciling science and spirituality was my conflict, not theirs. Both were comfortable with their own positions and had no need to have a discussion for my sake. Besides, I had never invited them to meet.

Quite recently, I had a startling experience. I was attending a special *yartzeit* (memorial) service at our temple for Rabbi Wine, three years after he had been tragically killed in an auto crash in Morocco. As part of the service, our music director sang "For Good," from the Broadway musical, *Wicked*. I was familiar with the words because two of our grandchildren had sung it to my husband at a party celebrating his 75th birthday. *Who can say if I've been changed for the better*, the lyrics go, **but because I knew you, I have been changed for good.** As I listened I simultaneously had two thoughts: one of Rabbi Wine and his intellectual brilliance, the other of Julia with her depth of spiritual wisdom. Images flooded through me showing how I had been changed by both relationships. Then, suddenly, not at all directed by my conscious mind, Sherwin and Julia took my hands, and each other's, and the three of us whirled in a circle together.

The inner debate was over and has never returned. The gap of that wordless longing I was never able to address through traditional organized Judaism is filled. I am no longer at the edge; I am at home in myself and in my Jewish life.

Epilogue: Sunlight and Gifts

Epilogue: Sunlight and Gifts

∽

It is August of 2008. I'm at my annual Summer Gathering in Ontario, a much anticipated week with a community of some 50 friends, all committed to spiritual deepening. On our fourth day, by common consent, we are honoring total silence. It is a ritual I look forward to each year. In the late afternoon sun, I feel a call to walk the labyrinth, a very large, carefully laid-out circular spiral of stones in the middle of a field of wildflowers. The spiral has many "dead-ends" and requires back-tracking in order to continue. Walking mindfully from the entrance to the center can take up to thirty minutes.

It is a custom to form a question as one enters, and then to pause at the center to receive an answer before beginning the spiral that takes one out of the labyrinth. I find that I have no question to ask. To whom or what I would address a question, if I had one, might be The Universe, angels, God, my Higher Self, spirit guides, inner wisdom, or other concepts that are abstract to some and very immediate to others. For myself, I don't know. I decide to simply walk, in a meditative state, and see whether a relevant question will occur to me.

I have been struggling for the past year to make sense of my diagnosis with a rare lung cancer (bronchoalveolar carcinoma, or BAC) which progresses very slowly. Because of the way it is scattered across my left lung, I am not a candidate for either surgery or radiation. Most chemotherapy is barely effective, I am told. There is one medication, a chemo in pill form, called Tarceva, but in over 70% of the eligible cases it doesn't work and has terrible side effects. It has been difficult for me to come to terms with this information. I feel perfectly healthy. Since the diagnosis, I have gone through anxiety, denial, anger and fear. I don't know how to think about or relate to the presence of the tiny malignant nodules in my left lung.

Because I have no symptoms, I've chosen to postpone treatment in favor of "watchful waiting."

The circular path before me is narrow, and to follow it I am forced to walk mindfully, one foot ahead of the other in a slow, meditative rhythm. The flat stones defining the maze-like pattern are overgrown with grass, weeds and wildflowers. Every few feet there is a low barrier and it is necessary to turn in a direction opposite from the one on which I imagined I was making progress. I walk and observe: tiny blue cornflowers, yellow buttercups, white Queen Anne's lace. Grasshoppers leap at my feet and cicadas sing. The sun is warm; tree branches wave in sudden gusts of wind.

Eventually I reach the center of the large circular area and stand quietly, waiting. At first nothing comes to me. Feeling disappointed, I am about to turn back. Two small bees buzz near me. I've spent almost seven decades fearing bee stings. Yet, not only have I never been stung, but a bee has never even landed on my skin. Such useless worry and fear! A thought comes: *These little creatures are just part of nature, doing their thing, nothing to worry about.* I relax and the bees move away.

And then the epiphany: *the little cancer cells are also just part of nature, doing their thing (dividing). They do not have to be the Enemy. We can peacefully co-exist.* They have been present for at least two years (and possibly much longer, one oncologist speculated). They have given me no trouble, have produced no symptoms, will likely not spread elsewhere in my body, and cause no pain. If the situation changes, I will get more medical advice and deal with it. For now, I can simply go on with my life, aware but not contracted around the issue.

The next thought arrives, equally unbidden: These little malignant nodules, encapsulated in the alveoli of my left lung, are *giving me a gift*. They have triggered an urgency about the years ahead that creates a new degree of aliveness in me. Because of their presence I have been motivated to complete unfinished projects, to appreciate the small blessings each day brings, to attend to inner space more frequently, to love more deeply. They have made me more keenly aware of both the beauty and the brevity of life. They are present to remind me to live fully in each moment. For these gifts, I feel gratitude.

This is more than a random thought. *It is a transformation in my psyche.* I feel a heaviness lift and a feeling of peacefulness and well-being takes its place in my heart. I give thanks and turn back on the slow but wondrous walk out of the labyrinth.

Because we are in silence until after breakfast the next morning, I have the opportunity to let this new awareness settle into me without pushing it away with conversation. In the evening I have supper in a state of contented silence. Then I walk slowly to the group room and peruse the wonderful notes, letters, articles and photos that others have left on the floor around the small table in the center of the room that serves as our altar. Finally, I drop into a deep meditation, then walk back to the Lodge and fall asleep early.

After breakfast, in our group circle, I share my experience with my friends. By now it is firmly part of me, as if weeks had passed rather than hours. Perhaps that's because the epiphany belongs to a dimension in which time is irrelevant. With loving faces, nods of understanding and, later, hugs of joy, my friends receive my story. I feel complete.

Four months later, in mid-December, I fall very ill with shaking, chills and exhaustion. I'm sicker than I ever have been in my 75 years on the planet. My internist tells me I have pneumonia and gives me an antibiotic. He doesn't believe anything will help the type of cancer I have and offers to call Hospice any time I need more assistance. I have no appetite and lose15 pounds. As the antibiotic takes effect, I slowly improve. But then, a few weeks later, a second bout of weakness and chills knocks me down even harder. On this round I spend time in a hospital and come home attached to oxygen 24 hours a day as the BAC nodules, activated by pneumonia, cut off my breath. For weeks I can barely speak or walk across a room. No one, including me, is sure I will survive.

But I do! Several factors bring me through this crisis. In the hospital I agree to begin treatment for the BAC with a new oncologist. Tarceva helps enormously and the side effects are minimal. The pneumonia clears and I'm slowly weaned off the oxygen tank. I receive tender, loving care from my husband and adult children as I lie on the living room sofa by day and in bed by night, weak and uninterested in food. Physically, palpably, I experience, both up close and at a distance, the love and concern of relatives and friends, including my entire spiritual community. I feel it through their phone calls, cards, e-mails, letters, gifts and nourishing home-cooked meals. When I think about them, visualize them as individuals or as a group, knowing they are sending their prayers and their caring, I tangibly feel my spirit lift.

And then there is Julia, who is able to transmit healing energy. Although Julia will not take credit for "doing" anything, I know that something flows through her to me continually, both from a distance and when she visits with me. It reaches my core in a way that is extremely powerful. I have no explanation for how this "works" and Julia offers none; it simply IS.

What is coming to me: the targeted medication, the love and prayers of others and the continual flow of energy from Julia, is only half the story. The other half is my own receptivity. I spend much time in silence, in a meditative state that I don't have to strive for, one that exists easily because of my lack of energy to do anything else. I have reached a state of surrender to whatever might be. Although I'm aware that death is a possibility, I find that I have no fear about the prospect. Rather, I feel a strong curiosity. I often think of the words of Julia's father, Mitch, just before he died at age 89, "I can't wait to see what the next adventure is." Like Mitch, I find it quite believable that there is another "adventure" into other realms of consciousness.

As spring approaches and my health begins to improve, friends ask me if I was bored or antsy being in the house all winter. The question surprises me; the answer is *No*. "Living in the moment" has become a given, no longer an abstract concept. I feel joy when the winter sunlight glistens off the unbroken snow and reaches through the window, warming me. I welcome lying on the sofa reading novels, something I generally save as an indulgence for summer beach vacations. When reading becomes too difficult, I nap with the sun on my face. I experience a strong sense of equanimity; there is nothing to accomplish; I can simply *Be*.

Weak and ill as I may feel, I'm not unhappy, but, rather, grateful every moment for the love that surrounds me. I pause each morning before I take my Tarceva to say a silent prayer of gratitude to those who developed it. I visualize the pill going directly to the cells in my lungs, and my lungs as clear and healthy. I experience myself one morning as expanding, my flesh porous, light and peacefulness flowing through me. The next day I have enough energy to put on my coat and go outdoors for my first short walk in three months.

By May of 2009, my CT scan shows my lungs to be clear, not a nodule in sight. Although I am concerned about radiation from such scans, I agree to re-check at intervals of 4-6 months. I'm back to my former energy, enjoying the fullness of life. Because I've been told that BAC is "incurable," I will continue to take my medication daily as maintenance, for as long as it works, which I hope will be measured in years. I strive to hang on to the many gifts embodied in the experience of my long winter, when the outdoor temperature was frigid and I was indoors bathed in sunlight. That memory continues to warm me as I move with renewed strength into the life still ahead.

About the Author

❧

Judith A. Goren, PhD, has enjoyed several careers, some simultaneously, over the past five decades. She has taught classes from 2nd grade to high school, as well as local adult education classes in Transactional Analysis (TA) theory and creative writing workshops. Concurrently, she and her husband, Bob, an attorney, were raising two sons and a daughter, and Judith was earning advanced degrees: a Master of Education (M. Ed) in Secondary Education, followed by a PhD in Humanistic and Clinical Psychology. Before and after the PhD she

developed a private psychotherapy practice with adults, working both with groups and individual clients. During these years (mid-60s to mid-90s) she was writing and publishing poetry as well as participating in poetry critiquing workshops. She and some of the participants have become life-long friends.

Born and educated in Detroit, Judith and Bob have always enjoyed travel, and during those decades of intense work and child-rearing, took frequent trips to other parts of the world, including Europe, China, Israel, Egypt and South America. Bob's life-long interest in pre-Columbian cultures has taken them to the sites of most of the major ruins in Mexico and Central America.

Their three children grew up, chose careers, married, and have families of their own: Gary (b. 1958) is an Administrator for the Alpena Intermediate School District, (ISD) in Michigan, comprising three counties; Steven (b. 1960) is a trial attorney; Nancy (b.1961) has a Master of Social Work degree (MSW), has worked as a therapist and a school social worker and is developing her talents in painting and in writing for young adults. Judith and Bob have nine grandchildren, each of whom is a source of love and joy in their lives. In December, 2011, they will celebrate their 58th wedding anniversary.

11045207R0

Made in the USA
Lexington, KY
05 September 2011